GRIEVING...
PERSONAL REFLECTIONS

GRIEVING...
PERSONAL REFLECTIONS

REUVEN P. BULKA

mosaic press

Library and Archives Canada Cataloguing in Publication

Bulka, Reuven P.
    Grieving-- personal reflections / Reuven P. Bulka.

ISBN 0-88962-817-3

    1. Grief--Religious aspects--Judaism. 2. Bereavement--
Religious aspects--Judaism. 3. Wives--Death--Religious aspects--
Judaism. I. Title.

BM645.G74B84 2005   296.7   C2005-903187-5

Publishing by Mosaic Press, offices and warehouse at 1252 Speers Rd., units 1 & 2, Oakville, On L6L 5N9, Canada and Mosaic Press, PMB 145, 4500 Witmer Industrial Estates, Niagara Falls, NY, 14305-1386, U.S.A.

Copyright© Reuven P. Bulka, 2006
Designed by Josh Goskey
Printed and Bound in Canada
ISBN 0-88962-817-3
Published by Mosaic Press

Mosaic Press in Canada:
1252 Speers Road, Units 1 & 2,
Oakville, Ontario
L6L 5N9
Phone/Fax: 905-825-2130
info@mosaic-press.com

Mosaic Press in U.S.A.:
4500 Witmer Industrial Estates
PMB 145, Niagara Falls, NY
14305-1386
Phone/Fax: 1-800-387-8992
info@mosaic-press.com

www.mosaic-press.com

ACKNOWLEDGEMENTS

I am grateful to all those who have contributed to this book, whether knowingly or unaware. Special thanks to my very dear colleague and friend, Rabbi Benjamin Blech, for his exceedingly generous foreword. And profound appreciation to Howard Aster and his crew at Mosaic Press, for putting it all together in such an elegant manner.

TABLE OF CONTENTS

FOREWORD

President John F. Kennedy won a Pulitzer Prize for his deeply moving Profiles in Courage. In it he came to a profound conclusion: "The stories of past courage...can teach, they can offer hope, they can provide inspiration. But they cannot supply courage itself. For this each man must look into his own soul."

Biblical commentators clearly agree with at least the first part of his observation. Why, they ask, does the Torah tell us tales of heroes when its primary intent is to serve as a book of law? The answer rests in God's desire not only to command us by way of teaching but perhaps more powerfully to transform us by way of epic example. Courage may seem humanly impossible unless we see it illustrated in lives of those we admire. Faith in the face of tragedy may appear unattainable unless we witness its reality in the biographies of people we consider our role models.

There is nothing more inspiring, nothing that can serve us better as source of hope for all of us as we face the challenges of our lives, than to reflect on the greatness of spirit achieved by those who were able to surmount the seemingly insurmountable ☒ and to offer us the inspiration of their example.

Small wonder that the same root word in Hebrew, Nes, serves for both the word test as well as the word miracle. To successfully master a divine test is no less than to demonstrate a human miracle.

That is why I stand in such awe of my friend and colleague, Rabbi Reuven Bulka. Forced to confront the unexpected death of his much beloved wife, a lesser man - even a Rabbi - might well have fallen apart personally and simply given up professionally. How did he do it? Where did he find his strength and his comfort? What can all of us learn from the way this Rabbi, who ironically had for so long written and taught about dealing with tragedy, actually demonstrated by his deeds how we can move from tears to acceptance, to growth and to greater spiritual awareness?

Thankfully my friend not only looked into his own soul, as Kennedy put it, but chose to share his most intimate thoughts with the readers of this remarkable journal.

This is a book that will long remain with you. It is sad, but at the same time it is joyful. It brings to mind the sage advice of King Solomon in the book of Ecclesiastes that "It is better to go to a house of mourning than a house of feasting." In the latter we escape from the realities of life; in the former we are moved to reflect on our ultimate values and the purpose for our sojourn here on earth.

I can only hope that readers will find as much to treasure in this work as I did. There is truly much wisdom in these pages, even as - remarkably enough - there is humour and the realization that in spite of everything, life is a gift from God that we all must appreciate. What Rabbi Bulka has accomplished is nothing less than a living sermon - a speech not of words but a lasting message of inspirational living.

Rabbi Benjamin Blech
Professor of Talmud, Yeshiva University

INTRODUCTION

This book is the chronicle of the passing of my dear wife, and the aftermath.

The chronicle shares with you, the reader, the range of emotions, the challenges, the difficult decisions, the reactions, that unfolded in this most trying time for our family.

Do Rabbis, or any clergy, grieve differently than others? Do they react differently to similar circumstances? Do their position and experience help, and if so, in what way? What words and gestures are most comforting?

These are the questions this book attempts to confront. If you are curious as to the conclusions, I can reveal that yes, rabbis grieve like everyone else, more or less.

But the experience of being a rabbi does create unique challenges, for better or for not so better.

All this I share with you, the reader, in the hope that these sharings will offer helpful, usable insights as we confront the inevitable whenever it comes.

Important Note

This book was written in the few months following my wife's death. It is now a few years since her passing. In that time, I have read and re-read the book, edited it, edited the edit, and agonized over whether I should publish it altogether.

My main misgiving is that the book is much too self-centered. And I hate that. Another misgiving is that some of my musings may seem like sour grapes, much ado about nothing. But it would have been difficult to write the book any other way.

In the end, with all the misgivings, I have decided to go forward, as is quite obvious. The only justification for this decision is that the book will make a useful difference for those who read it. Some of my most respected colleagues think that it will. I hope they are right.

Rabbi Reuven P. Bulka
Ottawa, 2005

THE CIRCUMSTANCE

The Peak

SUNDAY, NOVEMBER 5, 2000, was the happiest day in the life of an amazing lady, Naomi Bulka. I know this because I had the extraordinary good fortune to be married to this gallant woman for over thirty-three years.

Why was that day such a happy one? It was the day that her, more precisely our dear son Eliezer married a lovely young lady named Haviva Yeres. We have other children who are nicely married to great spouses - Yocheved to Moshe Shonek, Shmuel to Chani Hook, Rena to Yehuda Levy. We always loved our children equally, but Eliezer was different just by dint of circumstance.

A year prior to Eliezer's birth, we suffered through the death of our two month old son, Efrayim Yehezkel. He died of Sudden Infant Death Syndrome, commonly called SIDS. His birth was a great joy, coming after years of not being able to have children, a period of time in which Naomi suffered through a few serious miscarriages. So, when Efrayim was born, there was exhilaration in the air. And when he died, there was great despondency.

My wife was a resilient person, and though she was down, she was never out. She rebounded, and a year after the death of

5

Efrayim, Eliezer was born. Another equally precious child, Binyomin, came on the scene a few years later.

Binyomin, by the way, was at home during a critical time for his mother, and was an unending source of encouragement. All my children consider it more than fitting that Binyomin and his delightful wife Shira (Young) would be the first of the children to have a daughter after Naomi's passing, and who carries her Hewbrew name, Tzirel Nehama.

If for no other reason, Eliezer's wedding would have been a special moment. But there was an added dimension to the joy. Three years prior to Eliezer's wedding, Naomi was diagnosed with Breast Cancer. The news was crushing, but Naomi was determined to do whatever she could to fight this pernicious invasion of her body. She underwent surgery, and then endured a chemotherapy protocol of six treatments spaced at every three weeks.

By the time of the wedding, she was taking a low grade chemotherapy as a further preventive of recurrence, and had gone almost three years apparently cancer free. She had graduated from seeing her oncologist every three months, to seeing the oncologist every six months, and the visits were simply routine. Everything seemed well. The next visit was scheduled for just before the wedding, but Naomi decided to focus exclusively on the wedding, and rescheduled her appointment for the week after the wedding.

The day of the wedding, she was glowing on the outside and the inside. Her worry of three years earlier - will I be around for the wedding of my children, had now been relegated to insignificance. She was, after all, vibrantly there to experience the wedding of her miracle baby.

My wife did not usually interfere with the subject matter of my speeches. I have spoken under the wedding canopy at each of my children's weddings, and she enjoyed being surprised. This time, she made one request. It was that I should mention our and her gratitude for her being there. Needless to say, that was the most memorable part of my speech. I left it for the climactic conclusion, and did so in a way that gave vent to some very raw emotions.

As a matter of modesty, we never displayed overt affection in a physical manner in public. That day, she insisted on holding my hand, and when we took a picture together, it was with an unusually tight closeness. My dear wife was literally overwhelmed, swimming in a world of love and gratitude.

The Valley

A WEEK LATER, Naomi went to the doctor. Everything checked out well, except one test for liver function that yielded a higher than normal count. The oncologist did not think it was that significant, but nevertheless followed it up with a liver biopsy.

The results came back a few days later. They were devastating. The cancer had returned, and with a vengeance. A subsequent scan revealed that she had developed multiple tumours in the liver, five of them, each the size of a grapefruit. We were crushed. Just over six months later, on May 18, 2001, Naomi died. From the peak ecstacy of November 5, 2001, we went to the valley of utter despair, and in such a short time.

JUST BEFORE

A Critical Decision

ON THE FRIDAY of May 18, 2001, which was to have been Naomi's last day on earth, we were faced with a critical decision. The doctors at the National Institutes of Health were racking their brains. They could not understand why, after just a few days, Naomi experienced such a dramatic downturn.

They were frustrated, they were upset, but they were also determined to not rest until they could find the magic key to her regaining her health. In retrospect, by Friday the situation had deteriorated beyond repair. But we were all still in the fighting mode.

Toward mid-day, the doctors, a most dedicated team of top notch people, told me that they had done everything, but nothing was working and they were down to their last hope. This was to airlift Naomi to the Washington Hospital Center.

The logic of this was presented to me. At the National Institutes of Health, they were equipped to do angioplasty, which is what they suspected Naomi needed. They thought there was an arterial blockage which was at the root of the problem. Angioplasty can solve the blockage problem, but if the procedure does not work, the next step is a coronary bypass operation.

This they were not as equipped to do, but they were equipped at the Washington Hospital Center. And should that have become necessary, they did not want to lose the few hours of critical time that it would take to get her there.

Normally, an ambulance would take a patient from the one place to the other, but Naomi could not risk a mid-day traffic jam, or the bumpy ride. She needed to get there right away, and smoothly.

But first, I had to make a decision. Do I subject her to a further agony, a dislodging from the Intensive Care Unit at the National Institutes of Health, a helicopter flight with its inherent risks for someone in her condition, and an arrival and intervention at a totally different hospital. Or do I let things be, and allow the natural course of events to unfold?

To make matters worse, the doctors admitted that all this was a long shot, since they were not sure that arterial blockage was the cause of the body breakdown. But they had tried everything else, and this was the only plausible alternative which had a chance to make a difference. Hence, the option of helicoptering from the National Institutes of Health to the Washington Hospital Center, a very short trip.

I gathered all my children together, to listen to the doctors. We all asked questions about this, what were the up sides and what were the down sides. We then asked the doctors for privacy, to decide on this. One by one, the children observed that their mother never gave up in spite of what she was facing. They felt that they had no right to give up for her. This was exactly as I had felt, but I did not prompt them. I wanted them to be directly involved in making the decision. It was unanimous.

Naomi was flown to the Washington Hospital Center as quickly as humanly possible. The actual preparation for the flight from Bethesda took longer than the flight, since she had to be taken off all the machines she was on and connected to their more portable counterparts.

Fully anticipating that we would be in this new hospital for over the Sabbath, we took all our Sabbath stuff with us, namely the food for the Sabbath meals and basic clothes. Little did we know that the end was around the corner.

We rushed over by car, and came to the Washington Hospital Center not long after Naomi arrived. The doctors were again very caring and considerate, but they told us that the outlook was bleak. The arteries were not the problem, but there was nothing they thought could possibly turn things around. Naomi had flatlined and they had revived her, but they indicated that this would probably recur. It did, and they could not revive her.

As soon as I got any news from the doctors, I filtered it to my children, all of whom came over to the Washington Hospital Center. In between their fervent praying for the recovery of their mother, I had to truthfully let them know that it did not look good at all.

The moment that I had to tell them the bitter news, that their dear beloved mother was no longer alive, is firmly etched in my memory. I still hear the spontaneous explosion of grief. I still see all of us walking down to the room wherein she was being treated, to say goodbye, to say thank you to a most extraordinary wife, mother, daughter, sister, friend.

This was all so painful, but none of the children ran away from it. They confronted death head on, painfully but courageously. They had choices, but they chose the more difficult yet more direct path.

Involved Together

THE FACT THAT the children were involved in every aspect of their mother's last few days remains a source of great comfort to this very day. It was trying, but they would have had it no other way. Nothing could stand in the way of their doing whatever they could for their mother.

The devotion of the last few days was nothing less than a fitting manifestation of the devotion and love that prevailed throughout Naomi's lifetime. She was totally immersed in the lives of her children, and the children always reciprocated in kind.

It is so beneficial for everyone when the family bands together at a time of crisis. But it can hardly be expected that this coming together will spring out of nowhere. Closeness at the end is more likely to occur when there was closeness at the beginning, and in the middle.

Immediately After

A Break in Time

As MUCH AS we would like to write our own, made to order, exit scenario, the hard reality is that we cannot program death. Death comes at its own time, in its own place. Very rarely are we fully prepared.

Naomi died on a Friday afternoon, at the Washington Hospital Center, just two hours before the onset of the Sabbath. We were in an unfamiliar hospital, in an unfamiliar city. When I say we, I refer to all my children and their spouses, plus Naomi's sister from England, the sister whose stem cells were to have saved her life.

It was a race against time. We are prohibited from using a vehicle on the Sabbath, and likewise are enjoined from moving a deceased on the Sabbath via a vehicle. So, we needed to assure that Naomi would get to the Jewish Funeral Home before the Sabbath. The alternative of her being in the hospital morgue all through Sabbath was a less than ideal scenario. We also needed to get to a place before the Sabbath, so that we could observe the Sabbath.

The hospital staff, doctors and nurses, were extraordinarily helpful. They offered every form of assistance, including putting us up through the Sabbath in the hospital vicinity. We were very grateful. In the end, we succeeded in making the arrangements that assured her arrival at the Funeral Home minutes before the onset of the Sabbath. And, with the help of a nurse who knew the Washington area, we were able to get to the hotel for Sabbath, again just minutes prior to its onset.

The hotel was nowhere near any Jewish House of Prayer, so we were essentially "locked in" for the entire Sabbath. It was the first time in my life that I had been in such an island on the Sabbath, away from any synagogue, unable to pray with a congregation.

I was not happy about this, but I realized that there was no choice at the time, so we had to make the best of the situation. My children, God bless them, had already looked after preparing for the Sabbath, since we were already anticipating spending the Sabbath in the hospital, in Bethesda at the National Institutes of Health, not in Washington, D.C., at the Washington Hospital Center. The wine to usher in the Sabbath, the loaves of bread, and everything that goes into a traditional Sabbath meal menu, they were all on the table.

We were in different rooms, but we took the largest room and put together a few small tables to create a Sabbath table. Everyone at the meals remarked on how this togetherness in tragic times was so reflective of the family togetherness that was such a vital part of my wife's life. It was her great passion.

As I said, we cannot program death. With death, one learns to expect the unexpected. In my wildest dreams, I could not have imagined that as a consequence of my wife's death, I, who live in Ottawa, and my children, from New York, Baltimore, and Israel, would all land up in a hotel in Washington, D.C. for an entire Sabbath.

But this is exactly what happened. I would never recommend to anyone that, if they were able to write a death scenario, this is the way they should write it. Yet, looking back over all that transpired, I realize more and more what a great blessing derived from the hectic and nerve-racking circumstance.

We were stuck. We had no choices. We were alone together. And in that aloneness together, we, an already very close knit family, tightened the bonds of togetherness even more. We cried together, unabashedly. We reminisced together, affectionately. We talked heart-to-heart with each other, lovingly.

For over twenty-four hours, and allowing for some welcome sleep, we talked, we listened, we lamented, we extolled, we held each other tightly and warmly.

By the time the Sabbath had concluded, and we had to resume the hectic mode to finish all the necessary preparations for the funeral in Ottawa and the burial in Israel, we were simultaneously very sad and very energized for the tasks ahead.

The break in time that was forced on us by the Sabbath, with its uncompromising demand to avoid all manner of materially creative activity, forced us into a contemplative, reflective mode. What a great gift it was.

Though we cannot program the death scenario, we can take a page out of this experience. If, following death, there is a window of time, even an hour or two, I strongly recommend that the immediate family shut everything off for that time. No telephones, no faxes, no e-mails, no communication except with each other. It may be hard to create this time, but in the end the difficulties will be more than compensated for by what that time together will achieve - a tighter bond, to be in a better position to cope with the difficult moments to come.

The Best is More Than Good Enough

AFTER NAOMI'S DEATH in the Washington Hospital Center, we were faced with the challenge of taking care of arrangements prior to the Sabbath, about which I write elsewhere in more detail.

But the hospital was not without its own challenge. They wanted to do anything to help, but they were not conversant with the proper protocols of Jewish tradition immediately following death.

They did not know what to do, but they were determined to listen, to understand, and to implement. These were people who had little exposure to the type of situation we were in, but they more than compensated for the lack of knowledge with an eagerness to do the right thing.

That eagerness included even offering to drive us to the hotel where would be staying for the Sabbath, if that was the only way we could get there in time, prior to the Sabbath.

Consider this. These were busy nurses who were undoubtedly looking forward to relaxing on the weekend, and who were offering a bunch of strangers whom they had never before met and whom they would probably never meet again, a major chunk of their time.

In my capacity as Rabbi, I have often been involved in the preparation of guidelines for hospitals following the death of a Jewish patient. As important as having these guidelines may be, when one is caught up in the intensity of the moment, it can hardly be expected that the nurses will have the time and the patience to do a quick reading of the guidelines. And to expect the nurses to know the major nuances of the protocol following death for all religious groups is simply unfair. Nurses have enough to do, that we should not expect them to be theological thanatologists.

15

The most that we can expect is sensitivity to the particular religious demands of the hour. In our situation at the Washington Hospital Center, we were fortunate to be blessed with nurses who meant the best and who did their best. Their best was more than good enough. It was beyond praise. They facilitated every arrangement and meticulously carried out the fine details of Jewish law, as we outlined to them.

The move from the hospital to the Jewish Funeral Home was achieved with minimum complication and with maximum dignity.

Guidelines for what to do are helpful, but there is nothing more crucial for situations such as this than a caring and kind soul. The nurses had it, and we are ever grateful for that.

THE COMMUNITY SCENE

The Shock

MY WIFE'S DEATH came as a real shock. A shock, even though the prognosis was bleak. The shock reverberated all over the community. And it was partially my fault, because I gave the congregational community the impression that there was hope. I was not trying to fool them. I was conveying how I felt, how Naomi felt.

Her's was a serious cancer (which cancer is not serious?). The breast cancer which we thought had been eliminated metastasized in the liver, and in megadoses. She had grapefruit-size tumours, five of them, plus a proliferation of smaller ones. The outlook was grim. I do not subscribe to the medical practice of telling patients how long they have to live, and constantly urge those who have been given the death sentence to persevere through it, and go on with living.

But the best guesses of the doctors, as much as I did not like their making them, were for two more years, at most. Naomi was human. She did not react favourably to this, to say the least. But Naomi was also a super human being. The predictions did not deter her from pushing forward, taking control of the situation and exploring every possible avenue of cure.

This included looking into alternative medicine, not as an alternative to conventional medicine, but as a supplement. Naomi also encouraged her family and friends to pray for her. Jews and non-Jews all over the globe prayed for her, and fervently. Great sages were asked to bless her, and students poured over Jewish law in study that was dedicated to help effect recovery.

But the outlook remained bleak. A round of toxic chemo knocked the starch out of her. It was unlike her first encounter with chemo a few years earlier. Then she sailed through the six rounds of treatment with a minimum of side effects.

But then it was different. The chemo was a finite number, six treatments, no more, no less. She and I were excited when the protocol was completed. It was an occasion of great rejoicing. Goodbye chemo, goodbye cancer, hello life.

Until three years later, when the cancer resurfaced. Now, it was no more just finite chemo. It was endless chemo. There was hardly a hope that any chemo cocktail fit for humans could have eliminated her widespread cancer. We were into management mode. The best we could reasonably hope for was that the chemo would keep the cancer under control, so that at a later date, a cure might miraculously appear on the horizon.

Whether it was because this chemo regimen was of a different sort, or because her body had already been compromised by the previous chemo, this chemo lived up to all the warnings, eliciting every untoward symptom as foreshadowed in the descriptive literature about the drugs.

But Naomi remained confident, radiating faith and hope in spite of the horrific news. Every lead on frontier research was flagged, every glimmer of hope was investigated.

Then, by fluke, we came upon something going on in Baltimore. Our cousin, Dr. Joel Jakobovits, himself a distinguished physician, searched out this lead, but it led nowhere.

18

However, further research pointed to a Dr. Michael Bishop, who was in the midst of clinical trials at the National Institutes of Heath in Bethesda, Maryland, specifically on metastatic cancer.

We contacted Dr. Michael Bishop almost immediately, and as a first step, he sent to us the thirteen page detail of the proposed clinical trial. Naomi looked at it, and put it aside. I was not surprised, since I had read it prior to her reading it, and was pretty sure she would be scared away. The process was demanding, and the risks were quite high.

Things changed over the course of a very short few weeks. The chemo was getting to her, and the thought of going through chemo for the rest of her life was too much for Naomi. More and more, the Dr. Bishop option became more inviting. It offered no guarantees, but it offered hope.

The hope was a logical one. It called for a round or two of chemo, to just about knock out the old immune system, followed by a stem cell transplant that would effectively create a new immune system, a system which would recognize the tumours as foreign, and expel them. It had worked for other types of metastases, and Dr. Bishop and his crew were looking at the effectiveness of this approach for metastatic breast cancer.

The dangers were great. Aside from the affects of the chemo, there was the possibility of the body rejecting the new stem cells. This is called graft vs. host disease. It can lead to overwhelming problems.

We went down to Bethesda, to the National Institutes of Health, to meet with the good doctor and his team. They were terrific, then and throughout. Dr. Bishop laid out the dangers, leaving no room for misunderstanding. My wife was determined. She saw this as her only hope for a cancer free, chemo free life. Dr. Bishop accepted her for the clinical trial. Naomi was relieved, then alternated between trepidation and exhilaration at the prospect of full recovery.

We needed to find a match. That was easy. My wife's sister Hannah, from London, England, was a perfect match. Naomi's other siblings were all happy that a match was found, but somewhat disappointed that they could not be the life saver for their beloved sister.

Hannah came in from England to donate the stem cells, a process not without its discomforts. As well, Naomi gave a backup of her own stem cells just in case she rejected her sister's cells. We were now in full gear, and, most important from an emotional standpoint, we were in recovery mode. We were thinking about the clinical trial as the first step toward recovery.

By chance, we met a lady a few years younger than Naomi who had the same cancer, and was being treated at the National Institutes of Health with the same stem cell approach. She was a few months post-transplant, and doing nicely. That gave us even more hope.

When I bid adieu to my congregation in Ottawa, where I had been serving as Rabbi for close to thirty-four years, as we were about to return to Bethesda, I exuded the confidence that the treatment would live up to its promise. I would be down in Bethesda with Naomi for the few months following the treatment. She would need my constant presence just in case of an emergency, and would also need to make frequent follow-up visits to monitor her recovery.

Thankfully, the first round of chemo prior to the stem cell transplant had brought her levels down low enough that she did not need a second round. She proceeded straight to the pre-transplant chemo.

But by the time she was ready for the new stem cells, a few days after the chemo, Naomi was in trouble, in retrospect fatal trouble. She was having trouble breathing. She was taken to the intensive care section. There, in spite of intensive and loving care, she got worse. The stem cell transplant was administered when she was in quite difficult straights. But there was no choice. The stem cells had to be given then, or else the treatment would not work. Timing was essential, so that the taking over of the immune system by the new stem cells would come exactly as the old immune system was at its lowest point.

A day later, Naomi was induced into a heavy sedative state, to relax her body, which was fighting furiously to breath and to function. Nothing that was done, and they did everything, was able to get her out of this critical condition. She died just a few days after the stem cell transplant.

At the time, it was a cruel shock. In the space of a few days, we had gone from the focus on full recovery, to death.

Despair

THE AFTERSHOCK OF Naomi's passing was a painful despair felt by a grieving community comprised of loving family and a wide range of friends, from the congregational community, to her co-workers, and others who knew Naomi in different ways, mostly people she had helped and befriended in her usual quiet, unassuming manner.

Her funeral was unprecedented in the history of the community. There were upwards of two and a half thousand people in attendance, from all walks of life, from all faiths. The funeral took place in the synagogue she graced with her modest presence.

Appropriately, the funeral service was followed by a walk from the synagogue to Naomi's home, a short but long walk which gave the community further opportunity to convey its grief. From there, Naomi was driven to Toronto, to fly over to Israel for interment.

I was not aware until later, but many dignitaries descended upon the synagogue on the afternoon of the funeral. And it was only a few weeks later that I learned the funeral was a major news item that evening, both on radio and television.

The major local newspaper gave extensive coverage to the funeral, covering the first two pages of the City section.

What mattered most in the midst of the outpouring was the genuine grief that was clearly felt, and conveyed, by so many. This was, at the time, and continues to be, a great source of enduring comfort. To know that someone has touched so many lives, and has helped and inspired so many - these are profound feelings that have a powerfully consoling impact.

THE INTENSE MOURNING PERIOD

A Painful Remark

IN THE JEWISH tradition, the period immediately following burial is an intense period of mourning, called shiv'ah. Shiv'ah means seven, and refers to the seven days in which mourning is obligatory.

During this time, the mourners - parents, siblings, spouse, and children, sit either on the ground or on a chair that is low to the ground. This lowered center of gravity reflects the low feeling that those in mourning are experiencing.

Barring extenuating circumstances, the mourners are proscribed from leaving the home where mourning is being observed. The three daily prayer services are therefore held in the home of the mourners. In between regular prayer services, members of the community, family and friends, come by to offer condolences and bring comfort to the mourners.

In the course of this intense and sometimes tense period, it is almost inevitable that people will share a wide range of remarks and comments intended to offer comfort. What stands out in this regard is a comment in the form of a question, that was posed to me by a well-meaning friend - So, Rabbi, how does it feel to be on the other side?

This is a question that makes some sense when posed to a Rabbi who, after officiating at the weddings of many congregants, is now marrying off one of his children. It is a question to which a Rabbi can naturally, and happily, respond - it feels great.

But what can you answer when the question relates to how it feels to be the one who is in need of comfort rather than being the one offering comfort? I remember cringing on the inside, more out of pain than anger, when I heard the question, which was posed with nothing but good intentions.

What can one respond to such a question? That it feels great? This is obviously untrue. That it feels horrible? This implies that it feels good to offer comfort to others, and you would rather be doing that! As much as Rabbis offer comfort, they are not happy to do so. They must do so because of unfortunate circumstance, but they would all prefer that there be no such circumstance.

As is sometimes the case with complicated comments, this one refused to go away. At first, I could not get over the very nature of the question. But then, the sentiment of the question started to re-appear in comments made by others, such as - it must be hard for you to be on the other side, or the more benign - now it is for us to pay you back for your offering comfort to us on so many other occasions.

These are all well intentioned comments, which I greatly appreciated as the expression of sincere, caring sentiments. Even the comment, So, Rabbi, how does it feel to be on the other side?, was made with good intentions, even though it came out quite awkwardly.

As unwelcome as the original question may have been, actually sharing what it is like on the other side is not unwelcome at all. At least I hope it is not unwelcome. I hope that sharing the experience of the other side will not only help caregivers, clergy and others. I also fervently hope that it will help those who are trying, in the difficulty of role reversal, to help caregivers. Ultimately, I hope that what is revealed herein will help everyone in the way that grief is confronted.

Always Awake

IT IS TRUE that one needs stamina to help a loved one who is wrestling with a health crisis. It is also true that one needs stamina to persevere through a protracted mourning period.

In Jewish tradition, the period immediately following the funeral and burial is a time of prescribed intense mourning. It is called shiv'ah, meaning seven, since the mourning is for seven days. During that time, people come to visit the family, who sit on low to the ground seats, to offer their condolences and to reminisce about the deceased.

Considering how many people attended the funeral, it seemed most likely that the home where shiv'ah was being observed, Naomi's home, would be deluged from morning to night during the shiv'ah. Being available for almost a week of non-stop visits, from 8 in the morning to 10 at night, takes its toll. Of course, there is nothing wrong and everything right with taking a nap during the day, to recharge the worn out batteries.

But during the mourning period following the death of my wife, I resolved not to sleep at all during the day (not that I usually sleep during the day, although it is not a bad idea), no matter how tired I would be. Perhaps because of that resolve I never really became tired. It also helps to sit on hard, low to the ground chairs, as is the Jewish law for the mourning period. It is more difficult to wane into slumber on an uncomfortable chair.

Over the many years that I visited people during the post-burial week of mourning, it was somewhat frustrating to arrive at the house of mourning, only to be told that the mourners, or some of them, are asleep. This meant having to make a second visit, to see the asleep ones when they were awake.

So, fully cognizant of that, I made sure not to be asleep when anyone showed up. And it was a good resolution, since the visits to the house were effectively non-stop, from morning to night, over the entire official mourning period.

It would have been unfair for people to come, and for me not to be there. As it was, I did not sit with the family until the Tuesday morning following the Sunday funeral. This was because I accompanied my wife to Israel immediately following the Sunday afternoon funeral, for a second funeral service in Israel, and the subsequent burial, right next to our dear son Efrayim Yehezkel.

Not On the Phone

In anticipation of what I expected would be a torrent of telephone calls during the intense seven days of mourning called shiv'ah, I let it be known to family and friends who were answering the phone at home that I would not take any phone calls. I made it known that there were no exceptions to this, because if allowance were made for the exceptions, then everyone has a legitimate claim on being exceptional.

My children-in-law who answered the phone dutifully followed this directive, but wrote down the names of everyone who called. In the weeks following the shiv'ah period, I had occasion to speak with most of the 130 people who called.

Why was I so hard-nosed? And why do I share this with you? Had I taken all these calls, I would have observed the mourning on the phone, instead of sitting together with my family.

And being on the phone, I would have invariably either interrupted someone who was at the home for a condolence visit, or else would have made someone who had come to offer condolence sit and wait for my return from telephone conversation. To my mind, either alternative was rude, and therefore unacceptable.

But I would only recommend this if there is an anticipation of a phone call deluge so severe that it compromises the actual mourning observance. One or two calls from long distance relatives or friends who are close is not a serious interruption.

Finally, had I taken all these calls, my children, who themselves received a pile of calls from all over, would not have been able to use the phone!

Creative Condolence - Box of Strength

ONE OF THE most creative mourning visitations came compliments of a very caring, empathetic young lady. Without divulging names, this young lady, now in her teens, lost her father when she was quite young, and was eased into maturity by a very special Mom, who raised her in a most marvellous manner.

Needless to say, I had developed a very close relationship with the family over the years, starting from before the tragic passing of the father, when the going was good. The relationship intensified during the aftermath of the father's sudden death, and continues to the present.

27

This young lady came into the house, and sat down on a chair right in front of me. She smiled her natural, graceful smile, and then proceeded to hand me a note with a small box, the type in which one might put a ring, or earrings, or cufflinks. I wondered what this could be, since in general the mourning period is not gift giving time. In fact, gift giving is actually prohibited. But I did not want to in any way reveal a discomfort with her gift, so I took it.

The note was a wonderfully eloquent expression of concern, and in the note was a somewhat obscure reference to the contents of the box. It contained, in the words of this outstanding young lady, something of hers that she wanted to give to me; something very personal to help me through the difficult times.

I waited till later to open it, as was the young lady's desire. To my surprise, astonishment, and great appreciation, all the box contained was a piece of paper, on which was written the word "strength."

There was obviously much thought put into this, and much feeling. And it was felt. And it continues to be remembered.

Creative condolence is a most welcome gesture during what is a mourning experience that is more or less standardized. This is not to diminish from the usual mourning expressions, be they verbal or written. It is to emphasize that doing the unusual, in a thoughtful, respectful way, has a great and most beneficial impact.

Kids' Visits

Most parents, with the parental protective instinct always working, sometimes overtime, will be reluctant to bring their children to the house of mourning. They will want to shield their children from death and its aftermath.

Every parent has the obvious right to raise their children in what they think is the most appropriate manner. But before you make the decision not to bring your children, because you want to spare your children having to experience grief and pain, even if it is the grief and pain of others, let me share with you a personal observation.

There were many sources of comfort that came our way during the seven day intense mourning period, what is called the shiv'ah, and in the post-shiv'ah period. For me, one of the most comforting gestures was when parents came to the house of mourning with their children.

Why are children so comforting? For one, no matter what they ask, a child's question is by definition not a stupid question. Even a question which, if asked by an adult, would have qualified as a stupid question, would not be stupid coming out of the mouths of babes, or even teens, for that matter.

Adults who bring their children show that the entire family is affected by the tragedy. To hear a child, or a teen, express concern and sorrow is likewise to be inspired by the exciting thought that there is a caring generation coming after us.

And for a teen with whom you have worked when they entered into their coming of age via either Bar Mitzvah or Bat Mitzvah (the entering into responsibility for boys and girls respectively), to come and say - "you are more than my teacher, you are a person for whom I care;" that, dear readers, is a powerful source of comfort.

So, before you decide not to take your kids with you to a house of mourning where these kids know someone among the mourners, think of how comforting such a visit may be. And think, too, about how good your child will feel at having made a difference in the life of someone who needed a lift and received it via teen thoughtfulness.

Well Intentioned

As a way of tiding people over challenging encounters, we develop easy phrases for them. To open a conversation, we often start with "How are you?" Those who ask this are not always prepared for a detailed response. Try asking those who so enquire the following question - Which do you want, the 5 minute answer and the 1 hour answer?

Invariably, they want neither. Just a perfunctory, "fine, and you," will suffice. They use the phrase to launch into what they really want.

To close, we use another somewhat misleading phrase - I'll talk to you soon. How soon is soon? In some cases, soon is never. Another well worn exit phrase is "I'll get back to you." When, only God knows.

In leaving the presence of mourners, one often hears the words - May you have no more sorrow. I never liked this statement-wish, even though it is well intentioned. In fact, I never ever use that phrase when comforting mourners.

During the course of the mourning, I heard it hundreds of times. Each time I liked it less, at the same time as I deeply appreciated the genuine caring feeling that accompanied the statement.

When this statement was conveyed to me even by Rabbis who visited, I actually shared with them, in a non-confrontational manner, my concerns about the phrase. They will not be using it anymore.

It is nice to have a life free of sorrow, but in reality this means having a short life. No life can be free of sorrow. Sorrow is as much a part of life as eating, sleeping, and breathing. The longer you live, the more sorrow you are destined to experience. So, in a way that is the opposite of the intent, by wishing to someone that they have no more sorrow, you are wishing that they die soon.

Surely, no one means that. So, we should look for alternate expressions that are well thought out, that evoke sentiments which are consistent with one's genuine caring.

So, if "no more sorrow" does not cut it, what does? Try, as is my habit, the following - May you have many joyous occasions. Or, may you have a long life with many happy events, and the good health to enjoy them. These are positive sentiments, not only in sound, but also as translated into reality. There are of course many other possibilities, and everyone is free to compose phrases with which they are comfortable, and with which the mourners will likewise be comfortable.

Perhaps in anticipation of the difficulty people face in this regard, the rabbis of yesteryear composed a standardized exit formula. It goes like this - May the Omnipresent comfort you amidst the other mourners of Zion and Jerusalem.

This phrase links the mourners with Jewish history, and offers up the fervent hope that just as our history will be redemptive, so will our personal tragedy have a redemptive explication.

Being on the other side helped me see the wisdom of the Rabbis' approach, and sensitized me to the power of words, and how they creep into the mind and heart of the mourner.

Another important lesson in all this is that those who anticipate making a visit to a house of mourning should think in advance about what they will be saying by way of the opening or closing greeting. The conversation in the middle takes on a life of its own, but the opening and closing words are independent of the conversation. And they are words of immense impact. Therefore, mapping them out in advance is a sensitive and even necessary endeavour.

Post-Mourning Mourning

Was She Sick?

Often, after the conclusion of the seven day mourning period, I would get called from people who knew either me or my wife, or both, but were unaware about the circumstances, and caught by surprise. They would call to offer condolences, which of course were accepted with gratitude.

Then, in an attempt to place a better perspective on it, they would ask - was she sick? They do not say it outright, but often what is heard on the other side is, oh, she was sick beforehand, so that it is okay to die. To die out of nowhere is a problem; to die out of illness is acceptable and sometimes even a blessing.

I can almost guarantee that no one actually means this, or means to say this. If they did, it would amount to a futile, and senseless attempt, to give a positive spin to a negative reality. It does not work; never did, never will.

I admit to having asked this question to others in mourning, but have come to realize how discomfiting such a question may be. It is now removed from my range of possible questions.

If you ask the person who has just posed the question - do you mean to suggest that it was okay for her to die because she was sick, they will vehemently deny that this is what they meant. And usually it is true, that in their conscious thought processes they would never suggest that dying off illness is understandable, and therefore somewhat of a comfort.

But for many people, this is the way it sounds. Even before my wife's death, I had heard complaints from people who, during their mourning, were confronted with such questions. I would always try to downplay it, but having heard it so often in my own situation, I better appreciate why the question aroused such upset, even anger. At no time during the mourning period or after did I become angry, but I did get a better understanding for what arouses upset and anger in others.

So, my best advice on this matter is - do not go there. Do not ask - was she sick? Instead, say the following, or a variation thereof - "If you do not mind, I would be interested in hearing from you what exactly happened. If you are not in the mood, I understand perfectly."

Closure?!

WHEN I GREW up, closure was a political word. It was the procedure employed to cut off a filibuster in the United States House of Representatives or the United States Senate.

Today, hardly anyone is even aware that closure has political connotations. Closure is the psycho-babble term that is often used to describe the end of mourning, or the end to other unwelcome trauma.

My most incongruous encounter with this term came a number of years ago. A rampaging disgruntled former employee killed four other employees at the OCTranspo headquarters in Ottawa, home of the public bus transportation for Canada's capital.

The very next day, an item in the newspaper reported on efforts to have a memorial service for the four murdered OC-Transpo workers by the next week, in order, get this, that there can be closure!

It is one day into grief, and already the focus is on the end of grief, on closing off the emotional tap of melancholy. What are we anyway, machines that are turned on or off by some sort of psycho-switch?

Closure reminds me of everything skewered in the mourning process. Even the words "mourning process" leave a heavy psycho-odor. Mourning is mourning. It is not a process, a stage by stage endeavour somewhat akin to climbing a ladder to the roof. There are parts of mourning that are shared by many who mourn, other parts that are not shared. Some experience denial, others do not. Some take a few weeks to get back to a semblance of normalcy, others take more time, or less.

Loosely, we use the word closure to describe the feeling of having put the mourning away, and moving on. This only re-inforces a somewhat artificial approach to mourning, as a process by which one has to cycle through some unwelcome emotions. It is almost as if one has to give these emotions their due, and slowly but surely ease them out of the system, an elimination process of sorts, to close these emotions out (hence, closure), and then to live unimpeded by them.

Though those who patented the "closure" notion will vehemently deny that they intended this, still the way that closure is used in the media almost always signals a finality to the mourning, verily a forgetting of the past, and the one who passed away.

Closure runs directly in contradiction to a more meaningful approach to mourning, an approach which focuses on the gentle, delicate, but necessary move to "mourning towards," and away from the emotion of "mourning for."

In this approach, we never close off. Instead, we continue to remember, and slowly move from crying and melancholy to positive remembrance, via thoughts, behaviours and deeds that integrate and express the most noble values of the deceased. Instead of closing off the past, we open up a more meaningful future, based on the past.

ISSUES

Frustration

THERE WAS A great sense of frustration felt by many members of my Congregation, and by the larger community. How can we help? Everyone wanted to help, but they did not know what to do, how to help.

The truth is that there was not much that anyone could really do. But there were some who were clearly upset at this inability. And just sensing this frustration was a very comforting feeling. I would always make sure to share this feeling with the frustrated ones, that ironically their frustration was comforting.

But what could they do? Some offered that if at any time I "needed" to talk, they were there ready to listen. I heard this quite often, and did not doubt for one moment the sincerity of those who made the offer.

Our society has ingrained within us the idea that whenever there is a trauma, people need to talk it out. There is an assumption that everyone has some residue of feelings and emotions swirling around inside the soul, and failure to "let it out" can cause significant psychic damage.

That was not a concern, at least as far as I was concerned. I never was a "ventilator," and indeed I have many members in the congregation who are not ventilators. It goes beyond the Mars-Venus equation. I know many women who come to grips with their mourning quite directly, and have no need or desire to "let it all hang out."

It is indeed possible to make peace with reality without having a gut-spilling session. Some people may need it. But in my experience this need is usually associated with factors such as guilt, unfinished business, or complaints. I will proceed to address these three categories.

Guilt

GUILT OFTEN SEEMS to be interwoven in the fabric of mourning. Why did I not do this? Why did I not say that? Why did I not visit enough? And a host of other what might have beens had I done what I should have done. These thoughts often plague the mourner to the point that they impede the actual mourning. That is unfortunate.

We need to realize that we are all very imperfect human beings. We do not control life. All that can be expected of us is that we do our best. The fact that the best is frequently not good enough is irrelevant. Beyond doing our best, the rest is not in our hands. So what if it is possible that the deceased may still be alive had you not proceeded with a risky surgery. If the decision to operate was made in the best interests of the patient, that is all that really matters.

The imperfect nature of human life means that by definition we can never do enough. Once we accept this inherent, unavoidable limitation, we will be better able to handle the "if only I had done this or that" hypotheticals.

In our circumstances, there was not even a basis for guilt.

Every one of our children went beyond the extra mile. They showed their love and affection in so many ways, leaving no doubt about their feelings, and leaving no doubt in my wife's heart about these feelings. We expected and demanded nothing, but we received everything.

Every decision that was made was almost guilt free. The decision to embark on the experimental treatment, the clinical trial at National Institutes of Health, was made exclusively by my wife. No one could have, or should have made the decision for her.

We have no right to push people into high risk ventures, and certainly all the more so when life is at stake. All of us who were aware of the risks involved in the clinical trial shivered at the thought of it.

But once my wife decided to proceed, everyone was 1000 percent behind her, reassuring, hopeful, and fully supportive. If she could say yes to this heavy duty treatment, then that was the least we could do. And since it was my wife's decision, there was no reason to have any guilt pangs.

I am not sure, but there is a chance that Naomi would still be alive today had she not opted for the clinical trial. Then again, there is nothing in the early stages of the clinical trial that was any more invasive than the "ordinary" chemotherapy she would have been taking for her advanced cancer. And, I cannot say with any degree of certainty that she would have been better or worse off had she taken the route of unconventional therapies.

We thought long and hard about this, but in the end, Naomi was much more comfortable staying with convention, and supplementing with other helpful interventions, such as positive imaging and acupuncture.

In the end, it is really what the patient wants that must carry the day. It is the patient who has the cancer, it is the patient who endures the physical pain, it is the patient who must suffer through the chemotherapy and radiation with its unwelcome "side" consequences, it is the patient who knows best the limits of what is bearable, and it is therefore the patient who should make the ultimate decision, consistent, of course, with Jewish law.

Once the decision is made, with full awareness of the consequences, the supporting cast must fold in behind the patient, and offer unyielding, sustaining encouragement. This was done for Naomi in mega-doses.

Unfinished Business

UNFINISHED BUSINESS, THAT almost always comes up in conversations with mourners. If only we had an extra few hours we could have said this or that, done this or that. My wife and I had lots of unfinished business, as did all my children. My youngest son in particular had the unfinished business of his getting married without his mother at his side. My children have the unfinished business of their children's significant events, their graduations, Bar and Bat Mitzvah celebrations, their weddings, the birth of their children, which would have been Naomi's greatgrandchildren.

As for me, where do I begin? We did speak in the abstract on many occasions about how the passing of one's spouse should not deter the surviving spouse from remarrying. We often observed that a remarriage in these circumstances is eloquent testimony to how good the first marriage was. If the first marriage left much to be desired, why would anyone revisit this scene?

Of course, the conventional myth is that remarrying may even show disloyalty to one's deceased life partner. But conventional wisdom is often wrong, and this is one prime example.

But we never said goodbye, not I, not my children, not Naomi's parents, parents-in-law, not her siblings, not anyone. We never went over in detail what she wanted from me and her family after her passing. And I do not think I adequately conveyed to her how much I loved her, even though she knew.

The bald reality is that life is not a fairy tale. Smooth, well rounded, and complete endings do not usually happen. There is almost always unfinished business, and we must accept this as part of life.

There were a few glitches after Naomi's passing that could have been avoided had she told me. I refer to such things as papers and documents that I had to look for, lack of expressed direction or preference for the school our son should attend, etc.

So what? What is the big deal about spending a few more minutes looking? Every time I looked for something, I found other things on the way, interesting things. The search was worth it in and of itself. And my son and I worked out the best option for his schooling that his mother would have heartily endorsed.

Most important, when Naomi went on the trial trail, I simply could not get out of my mouth words such as - just in case, can you tell me this, that, or the other. It was infinitely more important for all of us to be positive, to talk the recovery talk, and to avoid at all costs talk about possible demise.

Does this mean that we were living an illusion? Does this mean we were living a fraud? Absolutely not. All it means is that we were uncompromisingly focused on Naomi's recovery. I will trade "finished business" for unabating optimism anytime.

41

And my own personal experience has definitely influenced the way I counsel others. I was always a big fan of optimism and hope, and am now an even bigger fan and advocate of being encouraging and offering hope, within the bounds of reason and reality.

Being on the other side has helped me to see even more clearly what is important on the other side of the other side.

Complaints

COMPLAINTS, LIKE GUILT and unfinished business, are a prevalent ingredient in mourning. Did we have complaints? Complaints to whom? The doctors? All of them, in Ottawa and in Bethesda, went through medical hoops to try to save Naomi. The nurses? They bent over backwards to help, to encourage, to push the healing process forward. In Ottawa, in Bethesda, in Washington, they were more than terrific.

Complaints to God? Why? Before voicing any complaint about Naomi's passing at so young an age, I would have to thank God for the thirty-three plus years of wedded bliss that we enjoyed together. But once I thank God for the thirty-three years, which I do, there is no room to complain.

This is a most vital lesson in dealing with tragedy. It is that complaints need to be presented in a balanced manner. The husband who complains to his wife for a supper that was late in coming, after many years of supper being served on time, is guilty of imbalanced complaining if he did not always express thanks for the on-time suppers.

The parent who complains to a child for a less than superb grade on a report card after never praising the usual high marks is likewise guilty of imbalanced complaining.

The boss who berates a worker for non-productivity, or for an error, but who never compliments the worker for the job usually well done, is another imbalanced complainer.

And the person who complains to God but never bothers to thank God is likewise guilty of imbalanced complaining.

In all instances of imbalanced complaining, there are victims. In the human interactions, the victims are usually the ones who are on the receiving end of the complaints. They suffer from the put down, and from the lack of any positive reinforcement when such reinforcement is so deserved.

The complainers, though not realizing it at the moment of complaint, are likewise on the way to becoming victims, victims of their own insensitivity. The imbalanced complainer will see the erosion of what could have been a flourishing spousal, parent-child, or employer-employee relationship, and suffers the consequences of that failure, together with the one who is on the receiving end of complaint. Divorce, alienation, tension at work and its attendant affect on work achievement, are all potential fallout from this imbalanced approach to voicing rebuke.

In the imbalanced complaining to God, it is the complainer who is the exclusive victim. God does not suffer or change because of the complaints, but the complainer is headed down the road to bitterness, nastiness, even renunciation of life. That need not happen, if only we realized and expressed our appreciation for the blessings we usually take for granted.

Questioning My Attitude

In the previous pages, I shared with you a glimpse of how I reacted to Naomi's passing. Privately, and occasionally publicly, I cried bitter tears for her, for her parents, for my parents, for her children and grandchildren, for her siblings, her friends, her congregation, and yes, for me.

But I had no complaints to God. Did I, do I have questions of God? I would be less than human if I did not. But questions is not the same as complaints. I still cannot make sense of it all. But I am not alone. There are so many people, inside my congregation, and beyond it, who endure pain and tragedy without knowing the why and the wherefore.

These are matters that we cannot know, and are perhaps better off not knowing. But we would all feel infinitely better if we knew that our loved ones were perfectly at peace in the loving embrace of God in heaven. Knowing my wife as I did, I am sure of this as much as I am sure of anything.

But you, the reader, are entitled to doubt my non-complaining reaction. How can I not complain when her death seems so unfair? How can I not complain when the tragedy sears a burning hole in the lives of all those who depended on her, who needed her?

And perhaps most pertinent, how do you know that I am reacting this way, or pretending to act this way, only because as a Rabbi this is what is expected of me?

I have not submitted to deeper analysis, nor do I intend to, to find out what resides in the inner layers of my feelings. I know that my reaction is perhaps related to my being a Rabbi only because being a Rabbi has forced me to confront the possible downsides of complaining. But it is a reaction that is desirable independent of who says it, or who experiences it.

Embracing a non-complaining approach in no way minimizes the depths of the hurt, or the extent of the mourning. What it serves to do is to make sure that the focus is on the mourning, on absorbing the full gravity of the loss, and not diverting to emotions that actually impede the mourning.

WORDS AND GESTURES

Thoughts With You

LET ME STATE THIS clearly and unequivocally, and to continually come back to this theme. I deeply appreciated every expression of condolence, no matter what the words that were used to transmit this, and no matter how far removed it was from the mourning period.

But I must admit that after a while a certain phrase started to wear thin. Perhaps it was because I heard it so often, perhaps because at some point in time it hit me at a weak moment and I began to question the meaning of the phrase, perhaps because, as some people have contended, I am much too literal, among other deficiencies.

For example, whenever someone mentions that so-and-so "had" a baby, I reflexively react by saying that so-and-so "has" a baby. Had is past, has is present. Crazy literalism at its best, or worst, depending on your perspective.

Back to the contentious phrase. That phrase is - my thoughts are with you. It sounds nice. Almost everyone uses it, yet I had a problem with it. As I reflected on it, I also realized that I had never ever used these words in extending condolences to others.

46

I may have used standard phrases like "I am sorry for your loss," I extend to you my heartfelt condolences," or "I wish you strength and health as you cope with your loss." But never, ever, words like "My thoughts are with you."

So, I asked myself whether I am the crazy one. Everyone seems to use this phrase, and I have trouble with it. What trouble anyway?

I have no proof, but I am pretty sure that this is a phrase imposed upon us by the greeting card industry. That is where you will see this phrase in block letters.

My problem with the phrase is the implicit distancing in it. "My thoughts are emanations from me, and they are with you." Why do we not use the more direct phrase - I am with you. Why is it that the thoughts are with the other, as opposed to the person being with the other? Would we ever say to our spouse - My thoughts love you? Or to someone in pain - My thoughts feel for you? These statements sound as goofy as they are.

We expect people to say to their spouses - I love you, or to those in pain, I feel for you. We expect them to be direct, to express how they feel, not how their thoughts feel.

So why, please tell me, do we create distance between the mourner and others by placing this artificial barrier called "thoughts" in the mix? The cynical side of me says that perhaps this is a subconscious reflection of the difficulty we have in handling grief, and rather than handling it directly, we let our thoughts do the handling. It gets us off the more direct hook. More likely, the aforementioned greeting card moguls needed to come up with a phrase that is catchy, that resonates with the public, that speaks to the situation but not too intimately.

However, there is a good chance that I am making more of this than I should, that there is no downside significance at all to the phrase - My thoughts are with you. The problem may in fact be my literalism.

Yet after all, I still think that there is something lacking in this phrase, and that we could do better. It is not a bad phrase, but there are more profound and meaningful phrases.

How about - My heart goes out to you? Maybe, but that too may not be as direct as we should be. How about not starting with "My," which is the source of the problem, and instead always starting with "I." The moment we begin with "My," we create the distance. It is not me that cares, it is my thoughts, my heart, my feelings. So maybe we need to shirk off the hesitancy to begin with the "I" word, a hesitancy rooted in our desire to be modest, to keep "I" in the background.

A few suggestions in this regard are - I feel so badly for you, I sympathize with you, I wish good things for you, I extend to you warmest condolences; even something so direct as - I am with you in your grief. This involves a change from the way we operate now, but it is, I hope, a change for the better.

As for those who use the "My thoughts are with you" phrase, rest assured that it is appreciated as a sincere comment expressing empathy. The desire in this as well as other observations on the words we employ is simply to bring the words we use into harmony with the sentiments we feel, to do the best we can, in the words that we use to convey comfort.

The better the words, the better the chance that the words will effectively conduce to soothing and healing. A little work on wordsmithing can go a long way.

Thinking of You

A corollary comment to "My thoughts are with you" is "I am thinking of you." Everyone likes to be thought of by others, I think. And to be told this does have a very positive impact.

Again here, I appreciated whenever this was told to me. I heard comments such as - I think of you every day, or I think of you often, or You are in my thoughts.

The linguistic sceptic in me has sometimes pushed me to thinking - am I that compact that I actually fit into someone's thoughts, however wide those thoughts may be? The crazy literalist strikes again!

And what about this "I am thinking of you" comment? When this comment is made, it is rarely followed up with a revelation of what exactly it is that the thinkers are thinking. For all you know, what they are thinking may not be all that welcome.

Yes, it is ridiculous to think that those who are thinking of you, and are kind enough to share this with you, are thinking untoward thoughts. But this misses the point. The point is that such language as "I am thinking of you" tells you nothing about the nature of the thoughts, therefore rendering such expressions as unnecessarily neutral. Again, I repeat that my difficulties with the phrase in no way lessened the great appreciation I had, and continue to have, for all those who shared their feelings via this phrase. It is just that we can do better, and because we can, we should.

So, what improvements can I recommend? The most obvious improvement is to go a step beyond "I am thinking of you," or "You are in my thoughts." What exactly are the thinkers thinking? Rather than sharing "that" they are thinking, would it not make more sense to share the actual contents of the thinking?

We need, therefore, to push this forward a bit. If the thought, or a variation of it, as it perforce would be, is - I wonder how he/she is managing, or I wonder if he/she is managing, then why not make this the comment. Hi, how are you? I am calling to find out how you are managing, and if I can help in any way?

Does this not ring more clearly? Does it not make more sense to actually express, in a definitive way, what exactly are the thoughts?

Here is another scenario. Let's say that the thoughts are thoughts of empathy. I know how much my friend loved his/her father, or his/her mother, or his/her spouse, or his/her child, or his/her sibling, how much a part of his or her life that person was, and how much of a gaping void there is in life now. How much more potent and consoling is a call in which this very thought is expressed, conveying to your friend that you can only imagine how much pain he or she must be enduring, and that you are calling to empathize with that pain, with that person.

The main point of all this is that as nice and acceptable as these comments about thinking of you may be, we can do better, and we do better by being more clear, more precise, more direct.

The more direct the language, the more likely that the language, and the person expressing it, will be a source of healing.   And after all, is this not what comforting mourners is all about?

No Magic Formula

MAGIC WORDS, HOW much we would like to have them. What a wonderful gift, to be able, with a few remarks, to comfort the bereaved, uplift the downtrodden, cheer up the depressed, encourage newlyweds, instill confidence in those who are approaching a major challenge, be it a new job, a critical exam, or an important medical test.

But we all know, or at least should know, that formulae work in math and physics and chemistry, but not in human emotion. If there were words that offered instant solace to the mourner, these words would have already long ago been packaged.

I could hear people struggle when they tried to comfort me. So often I heard people say words to the effect that "I wish I could do for you what you have done for so many."

This got me to think very seriously about that very statement. What had I done for so many? Only now, in the midst of mourning, did it hit me that people were actually comforted by me (and, I would hope, by any Rabbi or clergy). Yes, being a Rabbi in one community for over thirty-three years builds a sense of trust and closeness that is akin to extended family, and in some instances even closer than that. But ask me what I said or did to comfort, and I could not tell you.

I have no formula. I have no set prescription. I know what I avoid. I never say to a mourner "You should know no more sorrow." So many people, well intentioned, employ this phrase, but to me it is highly problematic, as I elaborate elsewhere (pp. 30 -31). Life inevitably has its sorrows, so to wish for no more sorrow is to wish for a shortened life. That is not the intent of those who say this, but it is the unavoidable consequence of such a wish.

I do wish the mourners long life and lots of happy occasions to enjoy it in good health and vigour. I do wish them that God grant them the strength to endure through the dark time. I do wish that the memory of their dear beloved be a source of comfort to them. But above everything else, what really matters is being with the mourners, not in a perfunctory way, but in a "I really want to be with you in your sorrow" way. That, to me, is the difference between clergy who do their job and clergy who make a difference. I do not know if I made a difference, but it sure was nice to hear that I did, no matter whether it actually was true.

Most Appreciated Words

OF ALL THE sentiments that were shared, there was one that I appreciated the most. Believe it or not, it was when people expressed a sense of futility that they did not know what to say. My feeling, when I heard these words, was - wow, this person really cares, and has grappled with a most difficult challenge, trying to find appropriate words.

I remember reading a book a few years ago by a woman who shared her experiences when she became a widow. She frowned upon those who came to comfort her and expressed their difficulties in trying to find the right thing to say. The theme of her negative reaction to this was something along the lines of - I have my problems, don't bother me with yours.

My reaction to those who shared how they were grappling was just the opposite. I took it as an honest expression of a sincere desire to be comforting but not finding the right way to do it. I took it as a lovely expression of serious contemplation, and in fact found great comfort in their inability to comfort.

I sometimes wonder whether there is something wrong with me, that I reacted in this way, after remembering the book on widowhood. But I remain firmly convinced that the accepting approach is the better one, since it is always better to appreciate than it is to denigrate. Besides, excessive focus on one's self during mourning, to the exclusion and even the dismissing of others, is counterproductive. It is more likely to cause the mourner to wallow in the mourning instead of working through it.

But you say, quite sharply, that I contradict myself by taking issue with the sense of the standard phrases used by those who comfort mourners. I know I am being repetitive, but I prefer repeat to misunderstanding. My comments about some comments to mourners are nothing more than hopefully helpful insights that fine tune the linguistic nuances of the shared condolences, that make a good thing better; we are dealing with suggested improvements, with upgrades.

The message in all this is somewhat surprising. It is that the most comforting of all words are the genuine admissions that the words are inadequate. Paradoxically, there is much adequacy in inadequacy, at least in the admission thereto.

Condolence on the Fly

THERE ARE A wide array of ways in which people express their condolences. The best, of course, is via face to face communication. There is something about the eye-to-eye, heart-to-heart connection that cannot be felt in any other medium.

But there are other, next best ways that can be comforting. The telephone is one, e-mail another, and cards yet another.

Cards or letters with well thought out messages have great value, in that they can be read and re-read, thus being a comfort that keeps on comforting.

Donations to charities in the name of the deceased also rank as a way to condolence, albeit less direct.

There is another quite prevalent form of condolence expression which gets not nearly the attention it deserves. This is what I refer to as "condolence on the fly." This is when the mourner, after having completed the seven days of intense mourning, and sometimes even long after, meets a friend, distant relative, or acquaintance for the first time since the death occurred. Such encounter is likely to begin with "Sorry about your loss," or "Condolences on your loss." It is a by-the-way type of consoling, not a going-out-of-the-way consoling.

I know more about this because it happened to me literally hundreds of times, perhaps because my wife's passing was in every media - on radio, on television, and in the newspaper. In a very real way, almost everyone in the city knew of it.

For the first few months, no matter where I ventured, someone would offer condolence. I took my son to the airport, and an airline attendant rushed up to extend her wishes. I took my grandson miniature golfing, and out of nowhere someone whom I knew was quick to express his sorrow. I went to the bank and everyone at the bank ran over to offer their sympathies. For a moment, I felt like an overdrawn customer who was being given a "what for" by chagrined bank workers. I would officiate at a wedding and guests would come over to express their sorrow.

Generally, I try to avoid creating expectations. This is for two reasons. One is that it is generally wrong to impose upon others what you think they should do. The other is that invariably if you expect whatever it may be from others, you are likely to be disappointed. So why pave the way for disappointment? There are enough disappointments in life without asking for more.

So, I did not expect a torrent of condolence, even though it came. And I certainly did not expect that whomever I met would preface any conversation with an expression of sorrow.

All those who do condolence on the fly mean well. Though at times it can be, and was, quite disconcerting, such as people rushing over to interrupt me when I was in conversation with someone else, in general the gestures are sincere, and were met with great appreciation, overtly expressed.

Making Excuses

THERE WAS ONE form of condolence on the fly that was somewhat irksome. This was when people would preface that condolence with excuses, such as the universal "I have been meaning to call you." Since I had no expectations, there was no reason to offer excuses. But of course, these people could hardly know that.

Yet somehow I could not help shut off the trigger in the brain which said to me - if you wanted to call, you had three or four months to do so, and it is only because you see me now that you react. Had you not seen me, you would never have called.

But, I said to myself, bite your tongue, and adjust your brain. People are busy, and they do not deliberately refuse to call. They simply get caught up in their activity and forget to call. So, accept graciously what they say, and react with appreciation. This I did.

But it would be wrong to leave this matter without one final comment. This is that if you know someone who has suffered a loss, and whom you may meet down the road, anticipate this and take the initiative. The quality of a sought out condolence is infinitely more appreciated than a condolence on the fly. And if for whatever reason you did not get around to it, it is better not to offer lame excuses such as "I was meaning to call you." The best excuse, if you feel you must offer an excuse, is the truth. I forgot. After all, we are mortal, we do forget, even things we have resolved to remember.

And if, for whatever situation, you are on the receiving end, accept the wishes with a positive mind frame and recognize that we are all mortals, and we sometimes err.

I offer this advice having been on both sides, and therefore fully aware of the upside of sought out condolence and the down side of condolence on the fly. Why be down when we can be up?

A Gesture to Be Remembered

A FEW MONTHS after my wife's cancer returned, and after the congregation became aware that we would be doing the shuttle to Bethesda on a regular basis, I received a visit from one of the members of the congregation.

He dropped by to leave a card with warm wishes from himself and his wife. This was greatly appreciated. But I was not prepared for what was in the card.

This couple, quite advanced in years and certainly not wealthy, placed an exceedingly large amount of money in the envelope with the good wishes. Luckily, though I opened the envelope after the visitor left, he was still in the building.

I ran after him, and expressed my thanks for the note and my astonishment at the many "notes."

He responded with two comments that I remember to this day. The first was that "you will have many expenses." The second was that they could never repay me for all that I had done for them.

I said thank you again, this time much more profusely, and went back to my office. I placed the envelope with the cash on my desk, right next to my computer. It is in a most visible place.

It is a few years since this magnificent gesture, and the envelope remains on my desk. I have not taken out the money. I must admit that on occasion I was tempted, but in the end nothing was so pressing as to remove what remains to this day a continual, inspirational reminder of an extraordinary kindness.

Overprotection

GOD BLESS ALL the people of my dear congregation. They did all they could to protect me.

For weeks after Naomi's passing, they shielded me from any problems, the normal day to day problems that Rabbis deal with. And they went so far as to discourage others from approaching me.

And I often heard others say that they were reluctant to call me because "I was dealing with my own problems."

Very nice, very compassionate, very understanding. Yes. But too much so. The intentions were nothing less than laudable. When I would hear of this, directly or indirectly, I would thank the person for their understanding. I would then proceed to tell them that as soon as the shiv'ah, the seven day intense mourning period was over, I went back immediately to "business as usual."

I made a conscious effort not to wait until I was ready to handle matters. I was afraid that in so doing I would never be ready. Remember the sage advice that is given to those who have just been in a car accident. They are advised to get right back on the road, the same way a child who has fallen off a bicycle is urged to get right back on it. Why? Because if you wait until you have recovered, you may never get back on the road, or on the bicycle. In the enforced waiting time, anxiety builds, and the move to get back on the road looms as an ever enlarging challenge.

That psychological insight goaded me to wade right back into the Rabbinical pool. And I also realized that this was not something that could or should be done in stages. The time to do it was immediately, and the way to do it was completely. You cannot be half committed. It is an either-or situation. Either all the way or no way. And no way was not an option.

In reality, getting immediately involved in the day to day matters was the best way to deal with life after intense mourning. Was I in the mood? No.

But if I waited to get into the mood, I would probably never reach that stage. Each day would offer another excuse to delay. And each delay would create a further distance from the embrace of responsibility, making the resumption of duties even more difficult.

HEALING

Who Heals the Healer?

THE ONE WORD answer to the question - who heals the healer, is - everyone. There are no magic words or magic potions, but every word or gesture that is offered helps. Every kindness inspires, every concern assuages, every thoughtfulness heals.

But in the end, the healer heals himself or herself, and so it should be. When the healer deals on such a regular basis with grief, as is the case in my circumstance, a mourning situation such as I faced becomes a challenge to authenticity.

If I do not listen to the words and ideas that I share with others in their grief, that renders everything I say as less than genuine, and bordering on the hypocritical. I have words of comfort and ideas for healing that are supposed to be good for everyone else. So why should they not be good for me?

I am mindful of the well known observation that "everyone can master a grief except he that has it," but remain unconvinced that this is absolutely true. More to the point is the Talmudic observation that a prisoner cannot extricate his/her self from prison. You cannot do it alone. You need help, from God, from people, from helpful ideas and ideals.

As I look back over the time immediately following Naomi's death, I find that the ideas I shared with others in their grief rebounded in a positive way on me. The most important notion in coming to grips with grief is that we are left with two choices, effectively an either-or. Either we capitulate to the grief, or we transcend it. Either we sink into depression and waste away life, or we confront life with renewed vigour.

There is nothing in between. We cannot be just half depressed and half enthusiastic. We cannot surrender partially and move forward somewhat hesitatingly.

I have often told those who are in a terrible state after the death of a loved one that what lies before them is this type of alternative, and that the worst way to memorialize the dear departed is to make their death be the cause of another death, a slow, painful, psychic, spiritual demise. This compounds the tragedy. The best way to memorialize is to be energized and inspired by the life of the one who has died, and to translate this into an even more meaningful life.

Confrontation with mortality that derives from experiencing death first hand is obviously traumatic, but it need not be permanently devastating.

Little Choice

IT TAKES TIME, time to go from the throes of despair in the immediate time after the death, to the moment when one realizes that there is no alternative but to respond by saying "yes" to life.

I knew almost from the beginning that confronting me was this very choice, which was a non choice. It was not only because I had a lovely bunch of children and children in law, grandchildren, parents, parents-in-law, siblings, and siblings-in law who would have been crushed had I chosen the depression alternative.

It was not only because I owed it to my congregation, and all those whom I visited during their mourning, to confront the future with requisite resolve.

It was because deep down, in the very core of my being, I knew that this was the only way to travel. I knew it not only because that is so essential a part of Jewish tradition. I knew it because I had seen, over the years, how the alternatives play themselves out, how choosing to affirm life is much more preferable to choosing to give up on life. Rebuilding offers a second chance at life; wallowing in depression takes down an entire entourage with the wallower.

Because I had seen all this, it did not take me long after the seven day intense mourning to move in that direction. Yes, I regressed on more than one occasion, breaking down at moments when the thoughts of what my dear wife had gone through and that she was no longer by my side ripped through my guts. But since I knew where I had to go, getting there was so much more accessible.

There is a message here for everyone. Having been forced to consider and confront grief long before experiencing it first hand, I was better prepared for it. And I am pretty sure that were I not in the clergy world, I would have done what everyone else does - push off any contemplation of the meaning of life, and the meaning of life after death, until it was foisted upon me by circumstance.

What would have happened then is anyone's guess. I really do not know, and cannot say for sure. I do know that living it out with others, writing a major book about it (Judaism on Illness and Suffering) a number of years ago, literally being forced to understand it, made it so much easier to meet the tragedy head on and move forward.

Grief Work

SINCE WE ARE all likely to confront death at some point or points in our lifetime, by which I mean the death of a loved one, it is wise to dedicate a set amount of time, long in advance of any tragedy, to contemplate all this, to be philosophically prepared, so that when the intense emotions subside, the strongly embedded philosophy can take over and steer you in the right direction.

Much has been said about the need to do grief work. To my mind, strange as it may sound, the best and most important grief work is done long before the grief, not afterward. It is realized through asking ourselves what we want out of life as well as what we are prepared to give to life. It is through asking whether we are sufficiently grateful for the gift of loved ones, and whether we are so spoiled as to demand that this gift be with us forever.

These are tough questions, and they cannot be asked in the throes of grief. But they can and should be asked well in advance.

FUTURE FOCUS

Moving Forward

IN GRIEF, WE are mired in the present and held back by the past. This is natural, and even justified. We are so overcome by the tragedy of the loss that we remain fixated on it, and for a time unable to move forward.

But there comes a time in every grief situation, a critical moment, when we break loose from the fixation, and move forward. This is not closure, this is not a purposeful forgetting of the deceased and all the past memories. Quite the contrary, it is the moment when we resolve to build on the past rather than be stifled by it.

It is the moment when our emotions catch up with the logical and unavoidable proposition that the greatest legacies we can bestow on the deceased are achieved through appreciation of the meaning and essence of the departed's life and how we can build on it. We then turn mourning into a futuristic endeavour. The accent is on how to perpetuate, not on how to lament.

The questions to be asked in this mind frame include - How can I best memorialize the deceased? How can I make myself into a better person as a way of honouring the deceased's memory? How can I make the world into a better place as a means to give the deceased's life some form of eternality in this world?

63

Once we start asking these questions, we have moved away from focus on the self, a focus which is entirely appropriate, and forward to the larger, meaning oriented issues. Some people take longer than others to reach this stage, but it is important to realize that this is the ultimate goal.

The goal is to give a positive focus to the tragedy, to transmute it into an opportunity to improve, and to improve the world. Lest you think that this is asking for the impossible, it should be noted that this is exactly what happens in most instances of grief, that the past is memorialized into the future.

What I am here suggesting is that we become more conscious of this, and to purposely make it happen rather than simply letting it happen.

In Memory of

THERE ARE SO many things we can do to memorialize a dear departed. There are high and low profile actions that all reflect the virtues of the deceased. These include charitable deeds undertaken in memory of, ranging from having a book donated to a library, to a building or hospital wing named after the deceased.

There are literally no limits to what can be done to perpetuate memory and to glorify legacy. Generally, though different people will approach this in their unique way, it makes sense that whatever is being done in memory should improve the status quo. It is one thing to slap a plaque on an already existing facility. It is quite another to create a facility in memory of. To improve the world in even the most minute way is a much more meaningful gesture.

With that in mind, many of Naomi's friends and admirers, and she had a host of them, got together to raise enough money to establish a Patient and Family Centre at the Ottawa Regional Cancer Centre. This center, which would not have been built otherwise, will go a long way toward easing some of the burdens of families coping with cancer. It is a most fitting tribute to her, as is the park and auditorium that was built in her name in Afula, Israel. Naomi loved kids, and was a superb kindergarten teacher before she got married, after which she built her own personal kindergarten.

There is another way to memorialize that does not get that much attention, but is nevertheless a most potent and powerful way to honour the memory of a loved one. This is in the form of resolving to improve one's own behaviour in honor of the loved one.

This can take many forms. It could be a resolution to give a small amount of charity every day. It could be to refrain from gossip or empty talk. It could be to set aside a dedicated time period daily for study. It could be to do a helpful deed at least once every day, ranging from giving your seat on the bus to someone who needs it more, to helping a child meet a challenge, to helping an elderly person eat supper.

These actions do not make headlines, but they make lifelines. And lifelines are more important than headlines.

Know Yourself

IN CONFRONTING THE aftermath of the mourning, it is important not only to have an awareness of some of the challenges. It is also important to know yourself, your strengths and your weaknesses.

Those who know me may find it hard to believe, but I can very easily lapse in laziness. I know this because I have done it. Every time I have an excuse to be lazy, I grab it. For example, whenever I finish writing a book, I take a long time before starting the next one. I use the convenient rationalization that I have just done something major (a real delusion), and that I therefore deserve a break.

It does make some sense to take time after the intense mourning before resuming one's normal life pattern. But we often do not have this luxury of time. I had the luxury. Had I gone away for a month, or two, the congregation would have fully understood. They probably would have been much happier than they were in seeing what they did. They saw me get back into the congregational and communal flow immediately after the conclusion of the seven day mourning period, the shiv'ah.

Some even expressed a concern that I came back too soon. As much as I appreciated their caring and thoughtfulness, I knew myself better. I knew that if I went away, I would easily acclimatize to the sedentary life. Getting back would have been all the more difficult.

I could not afford the luxury of waiting until I was fully up for the return. It never happens if you just wait. And I knew that there were not that many choices. Just two choices were available. Either move forward, or move backward. Staying in place, for me at least, was tantamount to moving backward. So, I decided to move forward. Looking back, I am not at all sorry that I did.

Dreading

I HAD NO problem with happy occasions. There were a number of joyous occasions slated for the weeks right after the mourning. I immersed myself in those just as I had previously. There was no pressure or ambivalence percolating inside me. I was happy for the families involved, and had no problem helping them enjoy those precious moments.

But I did have a dread. Believe it or not, I dreaded the thought of having to do a funeral. Funerals are to be dreaded at the best of times. After all, we would all prefer that family and friends are healthy and well. But I had what you would call a double dread, the normal dread plus the dread at the time.

Funerals, you say! That should have been easy. Maybe, if the need had presented itself, I would have done it. But I am really not sure how adequately I would have done it.

What was the problem with funerals? Simply speaking, I was emotionally drained on the down side, devastated at the loss of my full partner in life, my full partner in everything. I did not know if I could get sufficiently "down" for a funeral, to empathize with a grieving family, to properly lament the loss of life. For a month, I had no funerals. I was spared the challenge, so I will never know.

But I did make a point of going to hospitals to visit the sick. There was no dread there.

Hospital visits are standard fare for clergy. But the recent first hand encounter with illness left an indelible imprint on me, of the importance of visiting those who are not well.

Every such gesture helps lift up the spirit of those who are bedridden. And aside from good medical treatment, there is nothing that the unwell need more than they need a real spiritual uplift.

Almost everyone that I visited began their conversation with expression of condolence. And I could see from their body language that they were surprised that I was visiting so soon after the mourning period. And they were as appreciative as they were surprised. I knew that this would happen, that such visit would impact extra-positively on them. Which is why I made sure to do it.

Guilt Trip

IT IS ALMOST inevitable that in the process of getting back into the flow of life, some pangs of guilt will tickle the intestines. I am not talking about a massive, stifling guilt that is half way to depression. Instead, I refer to the small guilts that invade our consciousness on a sporadic, and more temporary basis.

These little guilt pangs surface when we are about to, or have just completed, a pleasant experience. It could be going to a concert, it could be having a gourmet meal, it could be enjoying an evening with friends. Why the pangs of guilt? Because you are enjoying something while the person whose death you are mourning cannot do the same.

Is it rational to think this way? Not really. But then, guilt is not really a rational emotion. Yet there is something to be said for this type of guilt pang, as long as it does not grow into an uncontrollable albatross. This type of pang shows a sense of caring, a feeling for others. It is not a punitive act, just a slice of hesitation. Hesitation is good, as long as this is all that it is. So, to hesitate before saying yes to a night out, before going to a ball game, is not so terrible. If hesitation becomes denial, then we are entering into a problematic domain.

Yes, I had these pangs. Not serious, but real. After the conclusion of the full thirty day mourning period, I could not get myself to listen to music. Was I allowed to listen? Absolutely. But I was not in the mood. So, for weeks after, I kept the car radio on the steady news and talk station, and kept away from classical music, which I normally love to hear.

Then, one Sunday, I had to make a three and half hour drive from Ottawa to Trenton, Ontario, for a special ceremony unveiling a plaque to honor the achievements, in war and in peace, of the 408 "Goose" Squadron. This is an heroic group that suffered tremendous losses in the Second World War, but fought with great courage and determination. In peace, it mapped Canada and continues to help with ice storms and other emergencies.

As luck would have it, the talk on the radio that day was nothing short of boring. I went from station to station, and everything was boring. Then, I said to myself - Go to the classical music station. But I hesitated. And then I started talking to myself. Why are you hesitating, I asked. And I realized it all had to do with Naomi. We always enjoyed listening to music when we drove long distances, which we did quite often. And now she was not there to listen with me.

But there is really nothing wrong with listening to the music, and at least by listening you will stay alert, I argued to myself. Besides, your children need you, and you cannot get into an accident. If you did, they would be shattered, and Naomi would be angry at you too, I concluded.

So, I made the move to the classical music station, and listened. It did not get me revved up, as it usually does, but it did keep me awake. And it paved the way for future listening. Chalk up another triumph for the 408 Squadron.

What the Deceased Would Have Wanted

WHAT THE DECEASED would have wanted. This is a most potent argument to tide us over the barriers to the return to life as it used to be. How often have I used this argument when meeting with the bereft survivors of a great loss. And I use this argument not as a technique, but as a true reflection of how best to approach life in the aftermath.

This is the usual scenario. Someone will be totally despondent after having suffered through a massive tragedy, and is not coping well; in fact, is coping miserably. Getting up in the morning is a chore. Going out and doing anything is the last thing that person wants to do.

If it sounds like depression, this is because it most likely is depression. But, I might add, understandable, perfectly normal depression. In fact, not to feel down is arguably less normal, whatever normal is supposed to mean.

This type of scenario is most likely to occur following the death of a spouse or a child. The world is dark and gloomy, with no sun on the horizon.

It is then that I weigh in, gently but firmly, with my argument that giving in, giving up, only serves to compound the tragedy. By the survivor dying ever so slowly through removal from being involved in anything, the original tragedy becomes a double death. That is not a worthy legacy for the deceased, or a fitting way for the deceased to be remembered.

In general, there is usually full agreement with this philosophical principle. The challenge is to move from agreement to implementation. So, I move to the next phase. I propose that the suffering survivors resolve to live as the deceased would have wanted. That would be the best way to honor the memory. What a fitting tribute it is to dedicate one's remaining years to the memory of the loved one.

70

Does this work? Sometimes, but certainly not all the time. Sometimes the depression is so great that medical intervention is needed. And there is no shame in this. A person being depressed is obviously a manifestation of human frailty, but it is a frailty which is at once a strength. It is the strength of genuine caring, and sensitivity to an intense connectedness that has been uprooted.

But it may sometimes be a case of too much caring, of an imbalance in the equation of life. It would be wrong to correct this imbalance by getting people to not feel pain altogether. The correct general approach is to place the caring into an appropriate and manageable perspective. To live as the deceased would have wanted offers the parameters for such a perspective.

The deceased would have wanted that life go on, that the surviving loved ones resume life fully and completely. That is the general motif. Based upon that, and deriving from that, are the issues that arise on a regular basis. Would Mom have approved of my choice of spouse? Would Dad have been happy if I skipped university for a year? Would my spouse be happy if I remarried? Would my child have wanted me to set up a scholarship fund honouring his or her memory? It is nice and fitting to include the projection of what the deceased would have wanted as one of the guideposts for our decisions.

Needless to say, this can also be abused in the opposite direction. I have observed some family members, usually children, conveniently proclaim that their deceased parent would have wanted them to do whatever, even though the whatever is totally inappropriate for the post-mourning period. But that is the exception. Most people take mourning seriously. We need to be sure they do not take it too seriously, too depressively.

In my own circumstance, my dear children did not leave me alone. For the weekend Sabbath times in the months following the death of their mother, they took turns coming up to be with me, to make sure I was not alone. Much as I would tell them that they did not have to turn their lives upside down, as they all had their own lives to live, they refused to listen to me. Instead, they insisted on listening to their mother, to the caring, enduring voice of a devoted wife, now no longer here, saying to them - take care of Daddy. It is certainly what she would have wanted, even though this was never explicitly stated.

REACTIONS

Vulnerability

DIFFERENT PEOPLE REACT differently after a personal tragedy. It is certainly not unusual for people in such circumstances to become edgy, irritable, and more likely to get upset.

Following the conclusion of the mourning, I found myself in numerous situations when I could have easily become upset. There were occasions when others expected me to become upset because they anticipated that this was the natural post-mourning reality.

Generally, I have a tendency to get upset, and at silly things. I get upset when two people engage in conversation going up or down an escalator, effectively blocking others who are in somewhat of a hurry from moving ahead. I get upset when people stop at a red light smack in the middle, blocking two lanes instead of one, thus making a right turn impossible. I get upset when people get on planes with obtrusive back packs that invariably hit innocents (me) sitting peacefully in their seats.

So, I was ripe for more upset. But I had a talk with myself. I told myself that I had just experienced a most devastating loss. Matters that would normally upset me are all trivial by comparison, and not worth getting upset. So, I told myself

- remember this whenever you sense that you are about to get upset. I worked on this for a short while, but it did not take long to win this internal battle. The logic was compelling. All that was needed was to remain cognizant of the logic.

Nothing Bothered Me

IT REACHED THE point when I could safely say that nothing of a purely material nature would dent my resolve to avoid becoming upset.

As good a posture as this may appear to be, it is not without its dangers. Carried to an extreme, you could end up in a situation wherein nothing bothers you. That is going a bit too far.

It is not healthy to reach the point that nothing really matters, a point that some who have been overcome by intense grief do sometimes reach. At that stage, one becomes anaesthetized to the world, oblivious to it, and eventually uncaring.

I do know that following Naomi's passing, when I was engaged in counselling with spouses who voiced what in perspective were trivial complaints but at the moment seemed so important, I would either say nothing and just look at them, or else I would say something along the lines of asking them to count their blessings, to feel gratitude for the simple fact that they had each other, and to see the complaints in the proper balance.

I would not dismiss the complaints as being unworthy of discussion. But I would be clear about the parameters within which the discussion should develop. And somehow, because they knew what I had experienced, the message had a more positive effect.

74

IMPACT

Does it Make You a Better Rabbi?

LOSING MY WIFE was a shattering experience for our entire community. Congregants, friends, even strangers, all felt the loss. I think that the shock of how quickly she died was a contributing factor. But more than that, they appreciated all the things she had done, in such a quiet way. Quiet people are hardly noticed, which is just the way Naomi liked it. But when they are no longer around, their absence looms larger.

When they are not around, it is as if the foundation of the building had been ripped out. You slowly begin to become aware of how much good was being done for you without realizing it. And you wonder what will be. Will life return to normal, whatever that means? Will life ever be the same? It can never be the same, that is for sure. And it certainly cannot be better without such a stalwart person who so unceremoniously looked after so many people and so many things, inside the family and out.

A worry that I heard from many was what effect Naomi's death would have on me. Would I be able to continue doing the things I do, but without Naomi? I knew this would be difficult, and it has been. But there are no other acceptable options. Never mind the obvious, the logistics of everyday life that we husbands often take for granted, such as the ready meals, the clean clothing, and the readiness to do things on the fly when they need to be done.

The biggest void is Naomi not being here. It is in missing what, via all the years together, had become us. When Naomi died, a big chunk of me went with her. It cannot be any other way when you live so closely bonded together for so many ears.

Gain in Loss

IN THE MIDST of all that has been lost, something has been gained. Perspective. I have a different, and hopefully better feel for the pain others are enduring. I understand better the pain that spouses go through when their partner in life is not well, and the outlook is bleak. I appreciate better the gravity of the loss of a mate.

Just before Naomi's situation had taken the sudden downward turn, I was involved with a lovely couple. The wife was battling a serious advanced cancer, and she was blessed with the great support of her loving husband, her devoted family, and an impressive host of great friends. She also had a terrific attitude, and a fighting spirit. In the end, the complications from cancer killed her.

Her husband, who was a tower of strength, was being battered from all sides. His mother had died just prior, his father was seriously ill, and in fact died shortly after his wife. Within the space of a year, he had lost both his parents and his wife. I thought I knew what he was going through, but I was wrong in that thinking. Only after having lost Naomi did I more fully appreciate the great impact of what he went through; more fully, but certainly not completely.

As much as we try to commiserate with those who have suffered a loss, it is almost impossible to fully grasp the crushing nature of the loss unless one has actually experienced it first hand. Yes, it is possible to be helpful, to empathize, to be a good friend. But to really understand, that is radically different.

I would be less than honest if I did not say that, given a choice, I would rather have Naomi and a lesser understanding. But now that she is no longer here, the least I can do is learn the right lessons and gain the correct perspective.

The Faith Factor

What Happens to One's Faith?

I HAVE SEEN people drawn to faith in the aftermath of tragic loss. I have seen people renounce faith in the aftermath of tragic loss. And I have seen a wide range of variations within these extremes.

As a result of going through grief myself, I better understand both reactions. I can see how, in the loneliness that is so inextricably linked with grief, one would seek solace in the comforting embrace of God.

And I can see how, in the devastation of losing a beloved, one would feel forsaken by God, and renounce faith.

In Jewish tradition, the person who has suffered the loss of a loved one (parent, spouse, sibling, child) is generally exempted from any religious duties until after the funeral. The more accepted rationale for this is that the surviving relative must be preoccupied with assuring the dignified farewell to the deceased, and nothing can be allowed to stand in the way. Even if the surviving relatives insist on being capable of fulfilling these religious duties, they are not allowed to do so.

I suspect that there may be more to this exemption than this rationale. It just may be that at the time of most intense

78

grief, one is not in the mood to do God's bidding, that one is angry at God. And that yes, God understands this, and mandates a brief pause to reflect that anger.

But it is only a brief pause. Because right away, immediately after burial, and in some places even on the way to burial, a doxology known as Kaddish is recited. The mourner expresses the yearning for the time when God's great Name will be universally sanctified. We do not allow the anger to last for more than a brief moment. There prevails a strong realization that precisely because understandable wavering from faith is likely, we enjoin the mourners to reconnect even more explicitly to faith.

It is not because God needs it. It is more because God knows that the mourners need it. For without God, without faith, there is not only loneliness. There is entrenched loneliness, what we would call despair, or a sense of being forlorn.

I have never seen a person of strong, unconditional faith, lose that faith as a result of a personal loss. The most vulnerable are those with a somewhat shaky faith, a results based faith. If the results are good, the faith continues on, but if the results are unwelcome, then the faith, rickety already, crumbles. But at the moment of greatest vulnerability, in the intense heat of grief, that is hardly the time for lessons in theology. That is more a time to allow the mourner some slack.

Making Excuses

And please do not ever say to a mourner - God took him, or her, because she was too good. First, one can never know why God does anything. Second, to suggest that being very good, or too good, justifies being taken away from this world, and sometimes being taken away amidst the turbulence of painful illness, stretches credibility. It is one thing to say that the deceased was an exceedingly good person. It is quite another to attribute the death to this.

It is somewhat absurd that the very thing we most aspire to in life, to be good, should be rewarded with death if you are too successful in being good.

Finally, if we really believe this argument, then anyone who survives alive is by definition not that good as to deserve to die. It is an insult to everyone, mourners, relatives, friends, anyone and everyone. So, beware of a praise for one that quite logically is a disparagement of everyone else.

It is through hearing these comments told to me, all by well-meaning people, that I have become much more sensitized, perhaps overly sensitized, to the meaning of the comments, and the implications of the comments.

MANAGING

How are You Doing?

HI. HOW ARE you doing? This is standard fare, a question that escapes our lips almost as a reflex. Most of the time, we ask it, and do not bother listening to the response. We have a talk show host in Canada's capital who hangs up on people who ask him this question. He claims that it is an absurd question, since the people asking really do not care, as they do not know him at all.

But this very question, posed in the days, weeks and months after the mourning, had a different ring to it. What do I say to this question? It is most difficult to answer. To tell the truth, to spill out all of one's feelings, that no one really wants to hear. To say something as inane as "fine" is to be somewhat inaccurate.

I started off by saying - thanks for asking. But most of the askers did not let me off that easily. You did not answer the question, they chimed. So I started responding to the question, How are you doing, by saying - doing. That did not resonate well. Then I tried saying - it is a hard question to answer.

Actually, many people, right after they blurted out the question, tried to rescind the question. They realized it was difficult to answer such a question. And now that I have experienced the question so many times, I refrain from asking it. It is unfair to place people into such an awkward situation.

Again let me emphasize that I appreciated every question asked, every concern expressed. That I learned, in the process, to avoid such questions is unrelated to how I felt about the question and the questioners.

I finally hit on a response to the question that worked to some extent. I said - no complaints. That seemed to work. Another was the old standby - Thank God. That is a well worn non-answer that somehow works its own magic. No one dares to question God.

But I am left with your question. If "how are you doing" does not make it to the top of the list, then what is an acceptable alternative? There are alternatives, but they ask of us to get into a more specific air space. Thus, one alternative is to remark on how you anticipate that things are not easy, and to ask - how are you managing the day-to-day responsibilities? This avoids questions that are related to feelings, and instead directs the focus to actions.

To that one can respond with what is hopefully the truth, and which addresses the question in a succinct way. It is easy to say - I am managing okay, or I am managing as best as possible under the circumstances, or other variations. The good thing about this question is that it transmits the feeling that there was thought behind it, that there is concern in it, and that there is genuine interest in hearing a response. All that is instantaneously comforting.

But "feeling" questions, they are tough to handle, both by the mourner and the consoler.

The Keeping Busy Diversion

MOST EVERYONE WILL agree with the importance of keeping busy as a way of dealing with mourning. If you keep busy, the logic goes, you will thereby keep your mind off the grief.

I would get calls from people asking me if I was keeping busy. The answer, forthright and accurate, was a yes. Then they would weigh in about how good, and important it is, to keep busy, and get your mind off the painful thoughts. They meant well, and I appreciated that they meant well.

But this too had an edge to it. The reminder of the "need" to get your mind off painful thoughts actually keeps your mind on them.

And it does not sit well to look at work as the necessary means to get your mind off the loss of a loved one. I certainly never went back to work in order to escape from thinking about Naomi. What a horrible thought, what a wrong way to handle grief.

Yes, it is more painful to meet this reality head on, but only in the short run. Over the long haul, deferring, putting off, avoiding, only makes matters worse, much worse.

I went back to work because there was no other viable choice, not as an escape. And, I have pictures of Naomi wherever I turn, on my desk, in the house, in my wallet, and most importantly, in my mind and heart.

Do we need diversions? Probably. But not for the commonly accepted reasons. The diversions are not for diversionary purposes, to avoid the issues, even though many people may do this. The diversions are nothing if they are not the necessary realities of life that we must return to after the tragic intrusion into, and diversion, from life.

To divert from the diversion is to get back on track.

A Few Calls

DURING THE COURSE of writing the first draft of this book, close to three months after Naomi's passing, I received a call from an old friend, someone who lost his wife after many happy years together. He called just to say hello, and indicated what many people had likewise mentioned when they called. This was that he had often gone to the phone to call, but stopped short of calling, because he was not comfortable with what he had to offer by way of conversation.

Finally, he said, he decided that if he kept on putting it off, he would never call, and that would be worse. As I mentioned elsewhere, I always appreciated calls, and specially calls like this, which were made with so much care and deliberation.

For those of you who deliberate so carefully, who hesitate before calling or visiting, and wonder whether you should share this with the person you are calling, my words to you are - do it. It has a sincere, comforting ring that resonates quite gently in the ears and heart of those you are trying to console.

Well, after this friend shared the context of his call, he proceeded to share with me how, after his wife's death, he valued being alone at home. He correctly assumed that I was being bombarded with entreaties from well-meaning people concerned about my being alone. He had gone through the same experience, though on a somewhat lesser scale, and spent a few minutes commiserating with me on what he correctly anticipated was happening.

I thanked him for his call. Little did he know how much this call was appreciated, not only because of the aforementioned sharing of the pre-call hesitation. It was because the caller, in his natural sharing, affirmed what I sensed in my own situation; that more than anything, I actually needed to be alone.

Does this mean that I wanted to withdraw from everyone? Not on your life. It was nothing more than a desire to be alone on certain occasions. To be alone is not necessarily to be lonely. And sometimes, when one desires to be alone but instead is in the midst of a group, however small, that can be very lonely. Loneliness is not a social phenomenon, it is a situational phenomenon.

On the same day that I received this call out of nowhere from the aforementioned friend, I had an interesting conversation with another individual, who reported to me on how much so many people wanted to do something for me. I realized from the get go that this was a problem, an unending source of frustration. I continually told those who pleaded with me to allow them to help that I really was a low maintenance guy. I never needed fancy meals. Tuna and lettuce was all I needed for my one daily meal.

Yes, that is all I usually eat, one meal, a light supper, daily. On the Sabbath and festivals I live it up, so to say, but other days, one meal is it.

Oh yes, there is the odd chocolate bar, or the tasty samples from the synagogue kitchen, but these are extras, welcome when they are available, yet not absolutely necessary.

But the frustration kept building. The person on the other end of the conversation told me how she was doing her best to "protect" me, telling people that I was okay, that I was best off not being bothered, that I actually preferred being alone at night, and yes, I was generally doing okay.

As much as I valued the fervent desire of so many to help, I valued even more this lady's understanding that sometimes the best help is in giving no help at all.

All this points to a most crucial matter in the way others relate to the person in mourning. Know the person, be ready to help, but be ready to help with what the mourner considers to be helpful, not with your own pre-conceived ideas of what help the mourner needs.

Please do not distort this as being ungrateful. At no time did I feel anything less than totally grateful. But being on the other side gave me glimpses of what is most helpful, glimpses which I share with you, the reader.

CHOICE

No Middle Ground

ONE OF THE more unexpected conclusions that derived from going through mourning, and which impacted on me more and more as time wore on, was, as I previously observed, that the choices mourners face are more realistically black-and-white choices, rather than grey choices.

Let me share with you a few examples. One example deals with the major issue, when and how to re-embrace life, an issue referred to earlier on. Hardly anyone really wants to rush headlong back into work. Given a choice, most would opt for an extended leave, to take care of unfinished matters, and to just chill out.

But most of the time, the option of taking a major block of time off is not available. The world does not wait for anyone, usually. And if you already have to get back to work, you need to focus at work. True, the people around you will understand, and give you some slack, but that does not mean you should automatically factor that in.

It is nice when such concern is offered without expectation. But if you rely on this wellspring of concern in advance, you will arrive back at work at best half-heartedly, and quite possibly with excess lethargy.

So, given that one must return to work, be it in the workplace, or in the home, what choices are there? Only two. One is to say no to life, to reject any re-embrace of life's responsibilities, and to withdraw into a black hole called depression. The other is to say yes to life, to re-enter life's arena with full resolve and uncompromising concentration.

There is really nothing in the middle. You cannot be just a little depressed, and just enough energized. Either you capitulate or you move forward. A little depression can easily become a big depression. And a half-baked effort, be it at home or at work, can feed on itself and become steadily worse.

No one can realistically be expected to return to work with the same energy level as before the tragedy. I am not advocating a gravity-defying approach. What I am suggesting is that once we realize the alternatives before us, and that there is only one really viable option, we will have an easier time sliding back into that mould.

Another black and white issue is the amount of intrusion coming from those who are genuinely concerned about you. Truthfully, there were times when phone calls were a pain, such as the third call on the line, with two others holding, insisting on taking me somewhere for supper. How long can I keep the others waiting? And why does where I eat supper become other people's business?

But, I say to myself - these people care about you, they mean the best for you, they desperately want to help. What you would really like is not too much concern, and not too little. To be ignored is crushing, to be overwhelmed is unmanageable, even stifling, but a golden middle is great. Great, but unattainable. It is out of our hands to be able to program how many people will be concerned, and how often they will show it.

There are two choices. Either there is concern around you, or there is not. Either you gracefully field all overtures to help, or you shut off, and shut the world out. Given the choices, it is obvious that the concern option is preferable. Once we accept that, we must accept all that comes with it - the intrusions, the time needed to field entreaties, and the alertness to express gratitude for all such expressions.

If we fully employ our grey matter on these issues, we will accept that there is little grey in these matters, that it is much more black-and-white. Once we realize that these are black-and-white challenges, we will have an easier time reflecting, and we will employ a more direct line of thinking that leads to the proper conclusion, the obvious choice of life in its fullness; because anything less would be the choice of its opposite.

Great Kids

I ALWAYS KNEW that I was blessed with great kids. After all, they had a great mother. She made them the center of her life, in an unimposing way. No matter what she was involved in, she always had the time, the eagerness, and the enthusiasm, to hear what they had to say about themselves, and about the grandchildren.

If you could devise a composite of what would constitute the ideal mother, you would probably come up with a Naomi clone.

When their mother departed from the world, they reacted in a way that would have made their mother proud of them, which indeed she was anyway. They refused to leave me alone. And I could not win. They insisted on being with me every weekend. They would not allow for me to be alone for a Sabbath.

So, every weekend, one of the kids came up, sometimes alone, sometimes with their spouse, sometimes with their kids. And not just to be there did they come. It was to come in advance, to prepare the meals, to clean up the place, to bring it up to their high standards of cleanliness, and to prepare enough to eat for the following week.

Every one of the kids was unique in the way they carried out their kindness. Which leads to an important point that I share with you. This is that you should invest wisely in your younger years. Put your energy into having as many children as you can, and love them to the full. My wife did that in megadoses, and I continue to reap the awesome benefits.

Do it without expectation of anything in return. It is almost guaranteed that you will not be disappointed.

PERSPECTIVE

The Monument

A FEW MONTHS after Naomi's passing, the Hakamat Matzayvah, literally the setting of the stone, erroneously referred to as an unveiling, took place in Israel.

For most of my children, this was doubly painful, since they had not travelled to Israel for the burial and this was the first time they actually visited the grave site of their mother.

Upon return from Israel, I was asked frequently - How did it go? What do you answer to such a question, well meaning as it may be? There is no answer. Is there such a thing as a good memorial service?

But there was a response that did resonate well, specially since it reflected the truth. I got into the mode of saying -it was a fitting tribute to her. It was.

Aside from the fitting tribute, events happening in Israel at the time helped put a perspective on grief. The week before, a mother in her thirties was shot by a drive by terrorist, leaving five young orphans.

The very next day after the Memorial Service, there was a horrific suicide bombing inside Sbarro's, a flourishing restaurant in Jerusalem, in which 15 people were killed, including one family of parents and some of their children, again leaving grieving orphans.

We had passed by Sbarro's just one half hour before the explosion, a chilling reminder of the fragility of life. And the surrounding tragedies were a reminder of the searing pain that other families are experiencing. In our own grief, we realized that we had so much for which to be grateful, that all our children had a loving mother for all the formative years of their lives.

In feeling, however remotely, the pain of others, one's own pain is placed into a more realistic perspective.

The Laundry

MENTION WAS MADE elsewhere of the great desire that so many people had to help in whatever way.

On one occasion, a pretty persistent lady buttonholed me, insisting that she had to do something, and would not leave me alone until I cooperated and gave her something to do.

I was stuck, and was forced to think of something that would at least qualify as an acceptable response, but which she would likely refuse. So, in what I thought was a brilliant retort, I said - you could do the laundry.

To my horror, she said - yes, gladly. Now I was in trouble. I fumbled my way through by saying that I was only joking, and that the laundry was being looked after. I learned how serious people were about helping.

There were others who knew my quirks and worked within them. They knew that I was not excited about eating in other places. During my life as a Rabbi, I made it a strict policy not to eat in any private home.

Since I did not know which home reliably adhered to the Jewish dietary laws commonly known as the Kosher Code, I resolved to eat no where. This way, I would not insult anyone by saying they were not "kosher enough."

Friday night Sabbath meals became a challenge. My children came up regularly, driving or flying from New York and Baltimore to Ottawa, but I asked them to stop doing so; not because I did not enjoy them, but because it was a great burden to them, though they would never admit it.

But there were many who could not fathom my eating alone on the Sabbath. So, they devised a nice ruse, whereby we would have a Sabbath meal in the synagogue right after services, which would be sponsored from week to week by families who wanted to join with me.

The ruse was that there were many families that were alone on Friday night who would welcome the opportunity to join with other families, to enjoy the spirit of the Sabbath together.

Whether or not this was true, I still do not know, but this is what they told me, to convince me to agree to this Friday night project. I agreed.

It started very small, with the first Friday night meal shared with four other families. The host for the first such endeavour was also the person in charge of arranging these Friday night dinners. It did not take more than a few days from after the first dinner before he was deluged with requests from people who wanted to be part of this.

And it quickly became a most welcome way to enjoy the Sabbath without making a dent in any of my quirks. And my gratitude to the folks who came up with the brilliant strategy remains intact.

A Better Year?

ABOUT FOUR MONTHS after Naomi's passing, the new Jewish year, 5762, loomed on the horizon. It was another gut wrenching time. People from all over called or wrote to wish the family well. The reminders were quite painful, as they all reflected on the difficult times.

As painful as the reminders were, they did bring a large measure of comfort, as the feelings expressed were so genuine and so full of caring.

Again, however, my ears started to play tricks on me. I heard something so often that it started to create a cringe. This was when people said, in a most well meaning way - I hope that next year will be a better year.

I started to ruminate on this. If someone had not been well in the past year, to wish that next year be better makes much sense. It is a wish for better health, for an improved condition.

If someone had a tough time, losing a job or losing money on investments, to wish for a better year also makes much sense. It is a wish that this year you find a job, or that this year the investments do better.

But if someone had died, how can next year be better? The only way it could be better is if the deceased comes back to life, but that does not happen.

And, as my youngest son remarked to me when I mused with him about this - how can this year be better? Last year, at least we had Mommy for more than a half a year. This year, we will not have her at all.

What a profound observation it was on his part. Indeed it cannot be better insofar as the deceased is concerned. As much as the sentimental wish for a better year derives from a genuine caring, it is an ill-conceived phrase, however well intentioned.

There are better alternatives. How about - I hope the coming year brings you good news. Or, I hope the new year will be fulfilling for you and yours. There are endless alternatives that are much more preferable to this problem laden wish.

FAST, OR NOT SO FAST FORWARD

Starting Over

IT WAS GOD Who said that "It is not good for the human being to be alone..." That remains a constant for all times.

One of the most painful steps that one is "forced" to contemplate following the loss of one's spouse is the prospect of starting over. Actually, starting over is the wrong term. More accurate is the term - re-embracing life.

For me, it was most excruciating. My family, all of whom took the loss of Naomi most painfully, urged me to take this step. They used the old argument that "Mommy would have wanted that."

In truth, we never talked about this in her later years. But we did muse about it in healthier times, and agreed that whoever survived, we would both want the survivor to re-marry, and not to remain alone. So, it was true that Naomi wanted that, and this knowledge helped get me going.

But the going was tough. I met a number of truly outstanding ladies. There are many out there. But I was not fair to them. I simply was not ready. I would spend much of the time talking with them about Naomi. To their credit, the ladies were all intent listeners, kind and considerate.

I did not go into this endeavour with illusions. I went in fully conscious of the absolutely inviolable rule that you never go into this seeking a substitute, a clone for your mate. On a conscious level, I did exactly that. But I could not help from veering into nostalgia, from comparing. And this was not fair. How can anyone compare? The Talmudic wisdom that "For everything there is a substitute, save the wife of one's youth," is an inescapable truth.

Starting over, with an intact family, is not the same as starting off fresh. And when I looked at my situation from a detached perspective, it dawned on me that anyone who would even contemplate this would have to be crazy, or close to it.

The overwhelming majority of eligibles are in the United States. For any of them to leave their own families to live in Ottawa is challenging enough. Add to the mix marrying a Rabbi who is hardly ever home, and as well instantly becoming a very public figure, and you can understand that contemplating this borders on lunacy.

I learned quite quickly that pre-conceived ideas of who is the ideal person in such a circumstance do not hold water. The elementary logic of the situation would have it that a widower is best off marrying a widow. After all, they both likely had good marriages and painful endings, and therefore would better understand each other.

Not so fast. Divorced women and never marrieds are not to be written off. It is the specific circumstance or situation that is critical, as is the warmth, kindness and understanding of the individual. These qualities are eminently present among divorcees and single ladies.

Twice Fortunate

As matters developed, I did meet a lovely lady named Leah, a widow from New York who lived right around the corner from one of my children, who was "crazy" enough to want to marry and move to Ottawa. We married a little less than a year after Naomi's passing. It was a chronological year later, but in reality it was a much longer period condensed into a shorter time.

Second marriages are loaded with great challenges, worthy of a book on its own. For any marriage to thrive, each one needs to work hard at it, and both need a measure of luck. For a second marriage to work, both need to work even harder, and both need even more luck.

In the instance wherein both partners are coming from having lost their first spouses, a critical matter is how the departed spouse fits into the new equation. To have a spouse who honours the memory of the new spouse's first spouse is a great blessing. How fortunate I am to have married a lady who maintains a great respect for Naomi, and through what she has heard, has gained a great appreciation of her, though she never met her.

Children too are a challenge, and Leah has developed a lovely relationship with my children, as I have with hers. The new spouse is not a parent, but is also more than a casual friend. To be able to find the middle ground, naturally and without imposing, is not easy, but Leah has done it.

The news that I was to re-marry caused quite a stir of excitement in the congregation and in the community. But, truth be told, there were some who felt negatively, that this was not an honour to Naomi's memory, that it was too soon, etc.

In Naomi's family, there have been a number of remarriages after very loving first marriages. It was understood that getting remarried is nothing less than a compliment to the first, departed spouse; that the marriage was so good that getting remarried is just the way to be.

Insofar as the matter of too soon, that is something that is entirely personal. Some people take longer than others to arrive at the point of thinking of remarriage. For some, family and personal circumstance are weighty factors in the process of moving forward. Barring the unusual, there is no right or wrong.

In the end, it is important to realize that marrying again is a reaffirmation of life. We mourn not to wallow in misery, but to more fully contemplate and appreciate the life of the departed, to take the lessons from that contemplation and weave them into life itself. Like the kaddish, the doxology which is recited after the death of the departed and which is an eloquent reaffirmation of faith, mourning is designed to lament toward a more meaningful future.

To wallow in misery because of the death of a loved one is to compound the tragedy. To reaffirm life after the death of a loved one is a profound compliment to the deceased. Remarrying following the death of one's spouse is an integral component of that reaffirmation.

CONCLUDING THOUGHTS

Reflecting back on the ruminations I shared with you in this book, I realize even more how much reason I have to be grateful.

I am grateful for the blessing of 33 plus years lived with an extraordinary lady, a lady of unbending commitment, uncompromising modesty, and indomitable courage.

I am grateful for the blessing of superb children, which includes their spouses, who are more children in fact rather than children in law.

I am grateful for the gift of outstanding parents and parents in law, again for whom the "in law" part is superfluous.

I am grateful for a vast array of dedicated siblings and their spouses, on my wife's side and on my side, but there really are no sides.

I am grateful for the support and understanding from my congregational community in Ottawa, for whom nothing was too difficult except the difficulty of having nothing to do in the way of helping out.

I am grateful for the outpouring of love and caring coming from literally thousands of people, family, friends, co-workers, even total strangers.

I am grateful for the wonderful legacy of memories that Naomi leaves as an indelible imprint on the lives of so many, within and outside the immediate family.

I am grateful to all those who in their own way contributed to the various projects that will further perpetuate Naomi's memory.

I am grateful for the ability to be able to focus on the many things for which to be grateful, and upon which to build for the future.

I am grateful for the opportunity to share my thoughts with you, and will be even more grateful if they help you, even in small measure, to cope with the unwelcome travails that we inevitably encounter.

And I am grateful for the recent blessing from God with which I have been graced, in the midst of abundant trans-generational blessings.

May blessing and gratitude crown all your lives.

MEMBER OF SCABRINI GROUP

Québec, Canada
2006